Federal Manual for Identifying and Delineating Jurisdictional Wetlands

AN INTERAGENCY COOPERATIVE PUBLICATION

Fish and
Wildlife Service

Environmental
Protection Agency

Department of
the Army

Soil Conservation
Service

January 1989

Federal Manual for Identifying and Delineating Jurisdictional Wetlands

An Interagency Cooperative Publication

U. S. Army Corps of Engineers

U.S. Environmental Protection Agency

U.S. Fish and Wildlife Service

U.S.D.A. Soil Conservation Service

JANUARY 10, 1989

For sale by the Superintendent of Documents, U.S. Government Printing Office
Washington, DC 20402

Federal Manual for Identifying and Delineating Jurisdictional Wetlands

We, the undersigned, hereby adopt this Federal Manual as the technical basis for identifying and delineating jurisdictional wetlands in the United States.

Frank Dunkle
Director
Fish and Wildlife Service

Rebecca Hanmer
Acting Assistant Administrator for Water
Environmental Protection Agency

Robert W. Page
Assistant Secretary of the Army
(Civil Works)
Department of Army

Wilson Scaling
Chief
Soil Conservation Service

January 10, 1989

Preface

This manual describes technical criteria, field indicators and other sources of information, and methods for identifying and delineating jurisdictional wetlands in the United States. This manual is the product of many years of practical experience in wetland identification and delineation by four Federal agencies: Army Corps of Engineers (CE), Environmental Protection Agency (EPA), Fish and Wildlife Service (FWS), and Soil Conservation Service (SCS). It is the culmination of efforts to merge existing field-tested wetland delineation manuals, methods, and procedures used by these agencies. This manual draws heavily upon published manuals and methods, specifically *Corps of Engineers Wetlands Delineation Manual*, EPA's *Wetland Identification and Delineation Manual*, and SCS's *Food Security Act Manual* wetland determination procedure.

The manual has been reviewed and concurred in by an interagency committee composed of the four Federal agencies. This committee was established for purposes of reconciling differences in wetland delineation procedures and developing a single interagency manual for identification and delineation of wetlands. The committee consisted of the following individuals: Robert Pierce, Bernie Goode, and Russell Theriot of the Corps of Engineers; John Meagher, Bill Sipple, and Charles Rhodes of the Environmental Protection Agency; David Stout, Ralph Tiner, and Bill Wilen of the Fish and Wildlife Service; and Steve Brady, Maurice Mausbach, and Billy Teels of the Soil Conservation Service. The manual was prepared by Ralph Tiner based on interagency committee decisions. The negotiations were facilitated by Howard Bellman and Leah Haygood.

This report should be cited as follows:

Federal Interagency Committee for Wetland Delineation. 1989. Federal Manual for Identifying and Delineating Jurisdictional Wetlands. U.S. Army Corps of Engineers, U.S. Environmental Protection Agency, U.S. Fish and Wildlife Service, and U.S.D.A. Soil Conservation Service, Washington, D.C. Cooperative technical publication. 76 pp. plus appendices.

Table of Contents

Part I.
Introduction

offered to provide users with a selection of methods that range from office determinations to detailed field determinations. If the user departs from these methods, the reasons for doing so should be documented.

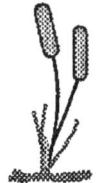

Purpose

1.0. The purpose of this manual is to provide users with mandatory technical criteria, field indicators and other sources of information, and recommended methods to determine whether an area is jurisdictional wetland or not, and to delineate the upper boundary of these wetlands. The document can be used to identify jurisdictional wetlands subject to Section 404 of the Clean Water Act and to the "Swampbuster" provision of the Food Security Act, or to identify vegetated wetlands in general for the National Wetlands Inventory and other purposes. *The term "wetland" as used throughout this manual refers to jurisdictional wetlands for use by Federal agencies.* This manual, therefore, provides a single, consistent approach for identifying and delineating wetlands from a multi-agency Federal perspective.

Organization of the Manual

1.1. The manual is divided into four major parts: Part I — Introduction, Part II — Mandatory Technical Criteria for Wetland Identification, Part III — Field Indicators and Other Available Information, and Part IV — Methods for Identification and Delineation of Wetlands. References, a glossary of technical terms, and appendices are included at the back of the manual.

Use of the Manual

1.2. The manual should be used for identification and delineation of wetlands in the United States. Emphasis for delineation is on the upper boundary of wetlands (i.e., wetland-upland boundary) and not on the lower boundary between wetlands and other aquatic habitats. The technical criteria for wetland identification presented in Part II are mandatory, while the methods presented in Part IV are recommended approaches. Alternative methods are

Background

1.3. At the Federal level, four agencies are principally involved with wetland identification and delineation: Army Corps of Engineers (CE), Environmental Protection Agency (EPA), Fish and Wildlife Service (FWS), and Soil Conservation Service (SCS). Each of these agencies have developed techniques for identifying the limits of wetlands for various purposes.

1.4. The CE and EPA are responsible for making jurisdictional determinations of wetlands regulated under Section 404 of the Clean Water Act (formerly known as the Federal Water Pollution Control Act, 33 U.S.C. 1344). The CE also makes jurisdictional determinations under Section 10 of the Rivers and Harbors Act of 1899 (33 U.S.C. 403). Under Section 404, the Secretary of the Army, acting through the Chief of Engineers, is authorized to issue permits for the discharge of dredged or fill materials into the waters of the United States, including wetlands, with program oversight by EPA. The EPA has the authority to make final determinations on the extent of Clean Water Act jurisdiction. The CE also issues permits for filling, dredging, and other construction in certain wetlands under Section 10. Under authority of the Fish and Wildlife Coordination Act, the FWS and the National Marine Fisheries Service review applications for these Federal permits and provide comments to the CE on the environmental impacts of proposed work. In addition, the FWS is conducting an inventory of the Nation's wetlands and is producing a series of National Wetlands Inventory maps for the entire country. While the SCS has been involved in wetland identification since 1956, it has recently become more deeply involved in wetland determinations through the "Swampbuster" provision of the Food Security Act of 1985.

1.5. The CE and EPA have developed technical manuals for identifying and delineating wetlands subject to Section 404 (Environmental Laboratory 1987 and Sipple 1988, respectively). The SCS has developed procedures for identifying wetlands for compliance with "Swampbuster." While it has no formal method for delineating wetland boundaries, the FWS has established guidelines for identifying wetlands in the form of its official wetland classification system report (Cowardin, et al. 1979).

1.6. In early 1988, the CE and EPA resumed previous discussions on the possibilities of merging their manuals into a single document, since both manuals were produced in support of Section 404 of the Clean Water Act. At that time, it was recommended that the FWS and SCS be invited to participate in the talks to take advantage of their technical expertise in wetlands and to discuss the possibilities of a joint interagency wetland identification manual. On May 19-20, 1988, the first meeting was held in Washington, D.C., to discuss technical differences between the CE and EPA manuals. After the meeting, it was decided that a second meeting should be held to resolve technical issues and to attempt to merge the two manuals and possibly develop an interagency manual for the four agencies. This meeting was held on August 29-31, 1988, at Harpers Ferry, West Virginia. Each of the four Federal agencies (CE, EPA, FWS, and SCS) was represented by three persons, with outside facilitators moderating the session. During the three-day meeting, the four agencies reached agreement on the technical criteria for identifying and delineating wetlands and agreed to merge the existing published methods (CE, EPA, and SCS) into a single wetland delineation manual. A draft combined manual was prepared, and then reviewed by the interagency group. On January 10, 1989, the manual was formally adopted by the four agencies as the recommended manual for identifying and delineating wetlands in the United States.

Federal Wetland Definitions

1.7. Several definitions have been formulated at the Federal level to define "wetland" for various laws, regulations, and programs. These major Federal definitions are cited below in reference to their guiding document along with a few comments on their key elements.

Section 404 of the Clean Water Act

1.8. The following definition of wetland is the regulatory definition used by the EPA and CE for administering the Section 404 permit program:

> Those areas that are inundated or saturated by surface or groundwater at a frequency and duration sufficient to support, and that under normal circumstances do support, a prevalence of vegetation typically adapted for life in saturated soil conditions. Wetlands generally include swamps, marshes, bogs, and similar areas.

(EPA, 40 CFR 230.3 and CE, 33 CFR 328.3)

1.9. This definition emphasizes hydrology, vegetation, and saturated soils. The Section 404 regulations also deal with other "waters of the United States" such as open water areas, mud flats, coral reefs, riffle and pool complexes, vegetated shallows, and other aquatic habitats.

Food Security Act of 1985

1.10. The following wetland definition is used by the SCS for identifying wetlands on agricultural land in assessing farmer eligibility for U.S. Department of Agriculture program benefits under the "Swampbuster" provision of this Act:

> Wetlands are defined as areas that have a predominance of hydric soils and that are inundated or saturated by surface or ground water at a frequency and duration sufficient to support, and under normal circumstances do support, a prevalence of hydrophytic vegetation typically adapted for life in saturated soil conditions, except lands in Alaska identified as having a high potential for agricultural development and a predominance of permafrost soils.*

(National Food Security Act Manual, 1988)

*Special Note: The Emergency Wetlands Resources Act of 1986 also contains this definition, but without the exception for Alaska.

1.11. This definition specifies hydrology, hydrophytic vegetation, and hydric soils. Any area that meets the hydric soil criteria (defined by the National Technical Committee for Hydric Soils) is considered to have a predominance of hydric soils. The definition also makes a geographic exclusion for Alaska, so that wetlands in Alaska with a high potential for agricultural development and a predominance of permafrost soils are exempt from the requirements of the Act.

Fish and Wildlife Service's Wetland Classification System

1.12. The FWS in cooperation with other Federal agencies, State agencies, and private organizations and individuals developed a wetland definition for conducting an inventory of the Nation's wetlands. This definition was published in the FWS's publication "Classification of Wetlands and Deepwater Habitats of the United States" (Cowardin, et al. 1979):

Wetlands are lands transitional between terrestrial and aquatic systems where the water table is usually at or near the surface or the land is covered by shallow water. For purposes of this classification wetlands must have one or more of the following three attributes: (1) at least periodically, the land supports predominantly hydrophytes, (2) the substrate is predominantly undrained hydric soil, and (3) the substrate is nonsoil and is saturated with water or covered by shallow water at some time during the growing season of each year.

1.13. This definition includes both vegetated and nonvegetated wetlands, recognizing that some types of wetlands lack vegetation (e.g., mud flats, sand flats, rocky shores, gravel beaches, and sand bars). The classification system also defines "deepwater habitats" as "permanently flooded lands lying below the deepwater boundary of wetlands." Deepwater habitats include estuarine and marine aquatic beds (similar to "vegetated shallows" of Section 404). Open waters below extreme low water at spring tides in salt and brackish tidal areas and usually below 6.6 feet in inland areas and freshwater tidal areas are also included in deepwater habitats.

Summary of Federal Definitions

1.14. The CE, EPA, and SCS wetland definitions include only areas that are vegetated under normal circumstances, while the FWS definition encompasses both vegetated and nonvegetated areas. Except for the FWS inclusion of nonvegetated areas as wetlands and the exemption for Alaska in the SCS definition, all four wetland definitions are conceptually the same; they all include three basic elements - hydrology, vegetation, and soils - for identifying wetlands.

Part II.
Mandatory Technical Criteria for Wetland Identification

2.0. Wetlands possess three essential characteristics: (1) hydrophytic vegetation, (2) hydric soils, and (3) wetland hydrology, which is the driving force creating all wetlands. These characteristics and their technical criteria for identification purposes are described in the following sections. The three technical criteria specified are mandatory and must all be met for an area to be identified as wetland. Therefore, areas that meet these criteria are wetlands.

Hydrophytic Vegetation

2.1. For purposes of this manual, hydrophytic vegetation is defined as macrophytic plant life growing in water, soil or on a substrate that is at least periodically deficient in oxygen as a result of excessive water content. Nearly 7,000 vascular plant species have been found growing in U.S. wetlands (Reed 1988). Out of these, only about 27 percent are "obligate wetland" species that nearly always occur in wetlands under natural conditions. This means that the majority of plant species growing in wetlands also grow in nonwetlands in varying degrees.

2.2. The FWS in cooperation with CE, EPA, and SCS has published the "National List of Plant Species That Occur in Wetlands" from a review of the scientific literature and review by wetland experts and botanists (Reed 1988). The list separates vascular plants into four basic groups, commonly called "wetland indicator status," based on a plant species' frequency of occurrence in wetlands: (1) *obligate wetland plants* (OBL) that occur almost always (estimated probability >99%) in wetlands under natural conditions; (2) *facultative wetland plants* (FACW) that usually occur in wetlands (estimated probability 67-99%), but occasionally are found in nonwetlands; (3) *facultative plants* (FAC) that are equally likely to occur in wetlands or nonwetlands (estimated probability 34-66%); and (4) *facultative*

upland plants (FACU) that usually occur in nonwetlands (estimated probability 67-99%), but occasionally are found in wetlands (estimated probability 1-33%). If a species occurs almost always (estimated probability >99%) in nonwetlands under natural conditions, it is considered an *obligate upland plant* (UPL). These latter plants do not usually appear on the wetland plant list; they are listed only when found in wetlands with a higher probability in one region of the country. If a species is not on the list, it is presumed to be an obligate upland plant. The "National List of Plant Species That Occur in Wetlands" has been subdivided into regional and state lists. There is a formal procedure to petition the interagency plant review committee for making additions, deletions, and changes in indicator status. Since the lists are periodically updated, the U.S. Fish and Wildlife Service should be contacted to be sure that the most current version is being used for wetland determinations. The appropriate plant list for a specific geographic region should be used when making a wetland determination and evaluating whether the following hydrophytic vegetation criterion is satisfied.

Hydrophytic Vegetation Criterion

2.3. An area has hydrophytic vegetation when, under normal circumstances: (1) more than 50 percent of the composition of the dominant species from all strata are obligate wetland (OBL), facultative wetland (FACW), and/or facultative (FAC) species, or (2) a frequency analysis of all species within the community yields a prevalence index value of less than 3.0 (where OBL = 1.0, FACW = 2.0, FAC = 3.0, FACU = 4.0, and UPL = 5.0). *CAUTION*: When a plant community has less than or equal to 50 percent of the dominant species from all strata represented by OBL, FACW, and/or FAC species, or a frequency analysis of all species within the community yields a prevalence index value of greater than or equal to 3.0, *and* hydric soils and wetland hydrology are present, the area also has hydrophytic vegetation. (*Note*: These areas are considered problem area wetlands.)

2.4. For each stratum (e.g., tree, shrub, and herb) in the plant community, dominant species are the most abundant plant species (when ranked in descending order

of abundance and cumulatively totaled) that immediately exceed 50 percent of the total dominance measure (e.g., basal area or areal coverage) for the stratum, plus any additional species comprising 20 percent or more of the total dominance measure for the stratum. All dominants are treated equally in determining the presence of hydrophytic vegetation.

2.5. (*Note*: The "National List of Plant Species that Occur in Wetlands" uses a plus (+) sign or a minus (-) sign to specify a higher or lower portion of a particular wetland indicator frequency for the three facultative-type indicators; for purposes of identifying hydrophytic vegetation according to this manual, however, FACW+, FACW-, FAC+, and FAC are included as FACW and FAC, respectively, in the hydrophytic vegetation criterion.)

Hydric Soils

2.6. Hydric soils are defined as soils that are saturated, flooded, or ponded long enough during the growing season to develop anaerobic conditions in the upper part (U.S.D.A. Soil Conservation Service 1987). In general, hydric soils are flooded, ponded, or saturated for usually one week or more during the period when soil temperatures are above biologic zero 41° F as defined by "Soil Taxonomy" (U.S.D.A. Soil Survey Staff 1975). These soils usually support hydrophytic vegetation. The National Technical Committee for Hydric Soils has developed criteria for hydric soils and a list of the Nation's hydric soils (U.S.D.A. Soil Conservation Service 1987). (*Note*: Caution must be exercised in using the hydric soils list for determining the presence of hydric soil at specific sites; see p. 12.)

Hydric Soil Criterion

2.7. An area has hydric soils when the National Technical Committee for Hydric Soils (NTCHS) criteria for hydric soils are met.

NTCHS Criteria for Hydric Soils (U.S.D.A. Soil Conservation Service 1987):

"1. All Histosols except Folists; or

2. Soils in Aquic suborders, Aquic subgroups, Albolls suborder, Salorthids great group, or Pell great groups of Vertisols that are:

a. somewhat poorly drained and have water table less than 0.5 feet from the surface for a significant period (usually a week or more) during the growing season, or

b. poorly drained or very poorly drained and have either:

(1) water table at less than 1.0 feet from the surface for a significant period (usually a week or more) during the growing season if permeability is equal to or greater than 6.0 inches/hour in all layers within 20 inches, or

(2) water table at less than 1.5 feet from the surface for a significant period (usually a week or more) during the growing season if permeability is less than 6.0 inches/hour in any layer within 20 inches; or

3. Soils that are ponded for long duration or very long duration during the growing season; or

4. Soils that are frequently flooded for long duration or very long duration during the growing season."

(*Note*: Long duration is defined as inundation for a single event that ranges from seven days to one month; very long duration is defined as inundation for a single event that is greater than one month; frequently flooded is defined as flooding likely to occur often under usual weather conditions - more than 50 percent chance of flooding in any year or more than 50 times in 100 years. Other technical terms in the NTCHS criteria for hydric soils are generally defined in the glossary.)

Wetland Hydrology

2.8. Permanent or periodic inundation, or soil saturation to the surface, at least seasonally, are the driving forces behind wetland formation. The presence of water for a week or more during the growing season typically creates anaerobic conditions in the soil, which affect the types of plants that can grow and the types of soils that develop. Numerous factors influence the wetness of an area, including precipitation, stratigraphy, topography, soil permeability, and plant cover. All wetlands usually have at least a seasonal abundance of water. This water may come from direct precipitation, overbank flooding, surface water runoff due to precipitation or snow melt, ground water discharge, or tidal flooding. The frequency and duration of inundation and soil saturation vary widely from permanent flooding or saturation to irregular flooding or saturation. Of the three technical criteria for wetland identification, wetland hydrology is often the least exact and most difficult to establish in the field, due largely to annual, seasonal, and daily fluctuations.

Wetland Hydrology Criterion

2.9. An area has wetland hydrology when saturated to the surface or inundated at some point in time during an average rainfall year, as defined below:

1. Saturation to the surface normally occurs when soils in the following natural drainage classes meet the following conditions:

   A. In somewhat poorly drained mineral soils, the water table is less than 0.5 feet from the surface for usually one week or more during the growing season; or

   B. In low permeability (<6.0 inches/hour), poorly drained or very poorly drained mineral soils, the water table is less than 1.5 feet from the surface for usually one week or more during the growing season; or

   C. In more permeable ($\geq$ 6.0 inches/hour), poorly drained or very poorly drained mineral soils, the water table is less than 1.0 feet from the surface for usually one week or more during the growing season; or

   D. In poorly drained or very poorly drained organic soils, the water table is usually at a depth where saturation to the surface occurs more than rarely. (*Note*: Organic soils that are cropped are often drained, yet the water table is closely managed to minimize oxidation of organic matter; these soils often retain their hydric characteristics and if so, meet the wetland hydrology criterion.)

2. An area is inundated at some time if ponded or frequently flooded with surface water for one week or more during the growing season.

(*Note*: An area saturated for a week during the growing season, especially early in the growing season, is not necessarily a wetland. However, in the vast majority of cases, an area that meets the NTCHS criteria for hydric soil is a wetland.)

Summary

2.10. The technical criteria are mandatory and must be satisfied in making a wetland determination. Areas that meet the NTCHS hydric soil criteria and under normal circumstances support hydrophytic vegetation are wetlands. Field indicators and other information provide direct and indirect evidence for determining whether or not each of the three criteria are met. Sound professional judgement should be used in interpreting these data to make a wetland determination. It must be kept in mind that exceptional and rare cases are possibilities that may call any generally sound principle into question.

Part III.
Field Indicators and Other Available Information

 **3.0.** When conducting a field inspection to make a wetland determination, the three identification criteria, listed in Part II of this manual, alone may not provide enough information for users to document whether or not the criteria themselves (i.e., hydrophytic vegetation, hydric soils, and wetland hydrology) are met. Various physical properties or other signs can be readily observed in the field to determine whether the three wetland identification criteria are satisfied. Besides these field indicators, good baseline information may be available from site-specific studies, published reports, or other written material on wetlands. In the following sections, field indicators and primary sources of information for each of the three criteria are presented to help the user identify wetlands.

Hydrophytic Vegetation

3.1. All plants growing in wetlands have adapted in one way or another to life in permanently or periodically inundated or saturated soils. Some plants have developed structural or morphological adaptations to inundation or saturation. These features, while indicative of hydrophytic vegetation, are used as indicators of wetland hydrology in this manual, since they are a response to inundation and soil saturation. Probably all plants growing in wetlands possess physiological mechanisms to cope with prolonged periods of anaerobic soil conditions. Because they are not observable in the field, physiological and reproductive adaptations are not included in this manual.

3.2. Persons making wetland determinations should be able to identify at least the dominant wetland plants in each stratum (layer of vegetation) of a plant community. Plant identification requires use of field guides or more technical taxonomic manuals (see Appendix A for sample list). When necessary, seek help in identifying difficult species. Once a plant is identified to genus and species, one should then consult the appropriate Federal list of plants that occur in wetlands to determine the "wetland indicator status" of the plant (see p. 5). This information will be used to help determine if hydrophytic vegetation is present.

Dominant Vegetation

3.3. Dominance as used in this manual refers strictly to the spatial extent of a species that is directly discernable or measurable in the field. When identifying dominant vegetation within a given plant community, one should consider dominance within each stratum. All dominants are treated equally in characterizing the plant community to determine whether hydrophytic vegetation is present. The most abundant plant species (when ranked in descending order of abundance and cumulatively totaled) that immediately exceed 50 percent of the total dominance measure for a given stratum, plus any additional species comprising 20 percent or more of the total dominance measure for that stratum are considered dominant species for the stratum. Dominance measures include percent areal coverage and basal area, for example.

3.4. Vegetative strata for which dominants should be determined may include: (1) tree ($\geq$5.0 inches diameter at breast height (dbh) and 20 feet or taller); (2) sapling (0.4 to <5.0 inches dbh and 20 feet or taller); (3) shrub (usually 3 to 20 feet tall including multi-stemmed, bushy shrubs and small trees and saplings); (4) woody vine; and (5) herb (herbaceous plants including graminoids, forbs, ferns, fern allies, herbaceous vines, and tree seedlings). Bryophytes (mosses, horned liverworts, and true liverworts) should be sampled as a separate stratum in certain wetlands, including shrub bogs, moss-lichen wetlands, and wooded swamps where bryophytes are abundant and represent an important component of the community; in most other wetlands, bryophytes should be included within the herb stratum due to their scarcity.

3.5. There are many ways to quantify dominance measures; Part IV provides recommended approaches. Alternatively, one may wish to visually estimate percent coverage when possible or perform a frequency analysis of all species within a given plant community. These are accepted methods for evaluating plant communities.

Field Indicators

3.6. Having established the community dominants for each stratum or performed a frequency analysis, hydrophytic vegetation is considered present if:

1) OBL species comprise all dominants in the plant community (*Note*: In these cases, the area can be considered wetland without detailed examination of soils and hydrology, provided significant hydrologic modifications are not evident); or

2) OBL species do not dominate each stratum, but more than 50 percent of the dominants of all strata are OBL, FACW, or FAC species (including FACW+, FACW-, FAC+, and FAC-); or

3) A plant community has a visually estimated percent coverage of OBL and FACW species that exceed the coverage of FACU and UPL species; or

4) A frequency analysis of all species within the community yields a prevalence index value of less than 3.0 (where OBL = 1.0, FACW = 2.0, FAC = 3.0, FACU = 4.0, and UPL = 5.0); or

5) A plant community has less than or equal to 50 percent of the dominant species from all strata represented by OBL, FACW, and/or FAC species, *or* a frequency analysis for all species within the community yields a prevalence index value greater than or equal to 3.0, *and* hydric soils and wetland hydrology are present. (*Note*: In other words, if the hydric soil and wetland hydrology criteria are met, then the vegetation is considered hydrophytic. For purposes of this manual, these situations are treated as disturbed or problem area wetlands because these plant communities are usually nonwetlands.)

Other Sources of Information

3.7. Besides learning the field indicators of hydrophytic vegetation presented above, one should also become familiar with the technical literature on wetlands, especially for one's geographic region. Sources of available literature include: taxonomic plant manuals and field guides; scientific journals dealing with botany, ecology, and wetlands in particular; technical government reports on wetlands; proceedings of wetland workshops, conferences, and symposia; and the FWS's national wetland plant database, which contains habitat information on about 7,000 plant species. Appendix A presents examples of the first four sources of information. In addition, the FWS's National Wetlands Inventory (NWI) maps provide information on locations of hydrophytic plant communities that may be studied in the field to improve one's knowledge of such communities in particular regions.

Hydric Soils

3.8. Due to their wetness during the growing season, hydric soils usually develop certain morphological properties that can be readily observed in the field. Prolonged anaerobic soil conditions typically lower the soil redox potential and causes a chemical reduction of some soil components, mainly iron oxides and manganese oxides. This reduction affects solubility, movement, and aggregation of these oxides which is reflected in the soil color and other physical characteristics that are usually indicative of hydric soils. (*Note*: Much of the background material for this section was taken from "Hydric Soils of New England" [Tiner and Veneman 1987].)

3.9. Soils are separated into two major types on the basis of material composition: organic soil and mineral soil. In general, soils with at least 18 inches of organic material in the upper part of the soil profile and soils with organic material resting on bedrock are considered organic soils (Histosols). Soils largely composed of sand, silt, and/or clay are mineral soils. (For technical definitions, see "Soil Taxonomy", U.S.D.A. Soil Survey Staff 1975).

3.10. Accumulation of organic matter in most organic soils results from prolonged anaerobic soil conditions associated with long periods of submergence or soil saturation during the growing season. These saturated conditions impede aerobic decomposition (oxidation) of the bulk organic materials such as leaves, stems, and roots, and encourage their accumulation over time as peat or muck. Consequently, most organic soils are characterized as very poorly drained soils. Organic soils typically form in waterlogged depressions, and peat or muck deposits may range from about two feet to more than 30 feet deep. Organic soils also develop in low-lying areas along coastal waters where tidal flooding is frequent.

3.11. Hydric organic soils are subdivided into three groups based on the presence of identifiable plant material: (1) muck (Saprists) in which two-thirds or more of the material is decomposed and less than one-third of the plant fibers are identifiable; (2) peat (Fibrists) in which less than one-third of the material is decomposed and more than two-thirds of the plant fibers are still identifiable; and (3) mucky peat or peaty muck (Hemists) in which the ratio of decomposed to identifiable plant matter is more nearly even (U.S.D.A. Soil Survey Staff 1975). A fourth group of organic soils (Folists) exists in tropical and boreal mountainous areas where precipitation exceeds the evapotranspiration rate, but these soils are never saturated for more than a few days after heavy rains and thus do not develop under hydric conditions. All organic soils, with the exception of the Folists, are hydric soils.

3.12. When less organic material accumulates in soil, the soil is classified as mineral soil. Some mineral soils may have thick organic surface layers due to heavy seasonal rainfall or a high water table, yet they are still composed largely of mineral matter (Ponnamperuma 1972). Mineral soils that are covered with moving (flooded) or standing (ponded) water for significant periods or are saturated for extended periods during the growing season are classified as hydric mineral soils. Soil saturation may result from low-lying topographic position, groundwater seepage, or the presence of a slowly permeable layer (e.g., clay, confining bedrock, or hardpan).

3.13. The duration and depth of soil saturation are essential criteria for identifying hydric soils and wetlands. Soil morphological features are commonly used to indicate long-term soil moisture regimes (Bouma 1983). The two most widely recognized features that reflect wetness in mineral soils are gleying and mottling.

3.14. Simply described, gleyed soils are predominantly neutral gray in color and occasionally greenish or bluish gray. In gleyed soils, the distinctive colors result from a process known as gleization. Prolonged saturation of mineral soil converts iron from its oxidized (ferric) form to its reduced (ferrous) state. These reduced compounds may be completely removed from the soil, resulting in gleying

(Veneman, *et al.* 1976). Mineral soils that are always saturated are uniformly gleyed throughout the saturated area. Soils gleyed to the surface layer are hydric soils. These soils often show evidence of oxidizing conditions only along root channels. Some nonhydric soils have gray layers (E-horizons) immediately below the surface layer that are gray for reasons other than saturation (e.g., leaching due to organic acids). These soils often have brighter (e.g., brownish or reddish) layers below the gray layer and can be recognized as nonhydric on that basis.

3.15. Mineral soils that are alternately saturated and oxidized (aerated) during the year are usually mottled in the part of the soil that is seasonally wet. Mottles are spots or blotches of different colors or shades of colors interspersed with the dominant (matrix) color. The abundance, size, and color of the mottles usually reflect the duration of the saturation period and indicate whether or not the soil is hydric. Mineral soils that are predominantly grayish with brown or yellow mottles are usually saturated for long periods during the growing season and are classified as hydric. Soils that are predominantly brown or yellow with gray mottles are saturated for shorter periods and may not be hydric. Mineral soils that are never saturated are usually bright-colored and are not mottled. Realize, however, that in some hydric soils, mottles may not be visible due to masking by organic matter (Parker, *et al.* 1984).

3.16. It is important to note that the gleization and mottle formation processes are strongly influenced by the activity of certain soil microorganisms. These microorganisms reduce iron when the soil environment is anaerobic, that is, when virtually no free oxygen is present, and when the soil contains organic matter. If the soil conditions are such that free oxygen is present, organic matter is absent, or temperatures are too low (below 41°F) to sustain microbial activity, gleization will not proceed and mottles will not form, even though the soil may be saturated for prolonged periods of time (Diers and Anderson 1984).

Soil Colors

3.17. Soil colors often reveal much about a soil's wetness, that is, whether the soil is hydric or nonhydric. Scientists and others examining the soil can determine the approximate soil color by comparing the soil sample with a Munsell soil color chart. The standardized Munsell soil colors are identified by three components: hue, value, and chroma. The hue is related to one of the main spectral colors: red, yellow, green, blue, or purple, or various mixtures of these principal colors. The value refers to the degree of lightness, while the chroma notation indicates the color strength or purity. In the Munsell soil color book, each individual hue has its own page, each of which is further subdivided into units for value (on the vertical axis) and chroma (horizontal axis). Although theoretically each soil color represents a unique combination of hues, values, and chromas, the number of combinations common in the soil environment usually is limited. Because of this situation and the fact that accurate reproduction of each soil color is expensive, the Munsell soil color book contains a limited number of combinations of hues, values, and chromas. The color of the soil matrix or a mottle is determined by comparing a soil sample with the individual color chips in the soil color book. The appropriate Munsell color name can be read from the facing page in the "Munsell Soil Color Charts" (Kollmorgen Corporation 1975). Chromas of 2 or less are considered low chromas and are often diagnostic of hydric soils. Low chroma colors include black, various shades of gray, and the darker shades of brown and red.

Hydric Organic Soils

3.18. Hydric organic soils can be easily recognized as black-colored muck and/or as black to dark brown-colored peat. Distinguishing mucks from peats based on the relative degree of decomposition is fairly simple. In mucks (Saprists), almost all of the plant remains have been decomposed beyond recognition. When rubbed, mucks feel greasy and leave hands dirty. In contrast, the plant remains in peats (Fibrists) show very little decomposition and the original constituent plants can be recognized fairly easily. When the organic material is rubbed between the fingers, most plant fibers will remain identifiable, leaving hands relatively clean. Between the extremes of mucks and peats, organic soils with partially decomposed plant fibers (Hemists) can be recognized. In peaty mucks up to two-thirds of the plant fibers can be destroyed by rubbing the materials between the fingers, while in mucky peats up to two-thirds of the plant remains are still recognizable after rubbing.

3.19. Besides the dominance of organic matter, many organic soils (especially in tidal marshes) also emit an odor of rotten eggs when hydrogen sulfide is present. Sulfides are produced only in a strongly reducing environment.

Hydric Mineral Soils

3.20. Hydric mineral soils are often more difficult to identify than hydric organic soils because most organic soils are hydric, while most mineral soils are not. A thick dark surface layer, grayish subsurface and subsoil colors, the presence of orange or reddish brown (iron) and/or dark reddish brown or black (manganese) mottles or concretions near the surface, and the wet condition of the soil may help identify the hydric character of many mineral soils. The grayish subsurface and subsoil colors and thick, dark surface layers are the best indicators of current wetness, since the orange-colored mottles are very insoluble and once formed may remain indefinitely as relict mottles of former wetness (Diers and Anderson 1984).

National and State Hydric Soils Lists

3.21. The SCS in cooperation with the National Technical Committee for Hydric Soils (NTCHS) has prepared a list of the Nation's hydric soils. State lists have also been prepared for statewide use. The national and State lists identify those soil series that meet the hydric soil criteria according to available soil interpretation records in SCS's soils database. These lists are periodically updated, so make sure the list being used is the current list. The lists facilitate use of SCS county soil surveys for identifying potential wetlands. One must be careful, however, in using the soil survey, because a soil map unit of an upland (nonwetland) soil may have inclusions of hydric soil that were not delineated on the map or vice versa. Also, some map units (e.g., alluvial land, swamp, tidal marsh, muck and peat) may be hydric soil areas, but are not on the hydric soils lists because they were not given a series name at the time of mapping.

3.22. Because of these limitations of the national and State lists, the SCS also maintains lists of hydric soil map units for each county in the United States. These lists may be obtained from local SCS district offices and are the preferred lists to be used when locating areas of hydric soils. The hydric soil map units lists identify all map units that are either named by a hydric soil or that have a potential of having hydric soil inclusions. The lists provide the map unit symbol, the name of the hydric soil part or parts of the map unit, information on the hydric soil composition of the map unit, and probable landscape position of hydric soils in the map unit delineation. The county lists also include map units named by miscellaneous land types or higher levels in "Soil Taxonomy" that meet hydric soil criteria.

Soil Surveys

3.23. The SCS publishes county soil surveys for areas where soil mapping is completed. Soil surveys that meet standards of the National Cooperative Soil Survey (NCSS) are used to identify delineations of hydric soils. These soil surveys may be published (completed) or unpublished (on file at local SCS district offices). Published soil surveys of an area may be obtained from the local SCS district office or the Agricultural Extension Service office. Unpublished maps may be obtained from the local SCS district office.

3.24. The NCSS maps four kind of map units: (1) consociations, (2) complexes, (3) associations, and (4) undifferentiated groups. *Consociations* are soil map units named for a single kind of soil (taxon) or miscellaneous area. Seventy-five percent of the area is similar to the taxon for which the unit is named. When named by a hydric soil, the map unit is considered a hydric soil map unit for wetland determinations. However, small areas within these map units may not be hydric and should be excluded in delineating wetlands.

3.25. *Complexes and associations* are soil map units named by two or more kinds of soils (taxa) or miscellaneous areas. If all taxa for which these map units are named are hydric, the soil map unit may be considered a hydric soil map unit for wetland determinations. If only part of the map unit is made up of hydric soils, only those portions of the map unit that are hydric are considered in wetland determinations.

3.26. *Undifferentiated groups* are soil map units named by two or more kinds of soils or miscellaneous areas. These units are distinguished from the others in that "and" is used as a conjunction in the name, while dashes are used for complexes and associations. If all components are hydric, the map

unit may be considered a hydric soil map unit. If one or more of the soils for which the unit is named are nonhydric, each area must be examined for the presence of hydric soils.

Use of the Hydric Soils List and Soil Surveys

3.27. The hydric soils list and county soil surveys may be used to help determine if the hydric soil criterion is met in a given area. When making a wetland determination, one should first locate the area of concern on a soil survey map and identify the soil map units for the area. The list of hydric soils should be consulted to determine whether the soil map units are hydric. If hydric soil map units are noted, then one should examine the soil in the field and compare its morphology with the corresponding hydric soil description in the soil survey report. If the soil's characteristics match those described for hydric soil, then the hydric soil criterion is met, unless the soil has been effectively drained (see disturbed areas section, p. 50). In the absence of site-specific information, hydric soils also may be recognized by field indicators.

Field Indicators

3.28. Several field indicators are available for determining whether a given soil meets the definition and criteria for hydric soils. Other factors to consider in recognizing hydric soils include obligate wetland plants, topography, observed or recorded inundation or soil saturation, and evidence of human alterations, e.g., drainage and filling. Any one of the following may indicate that hydric soils are present:

1) *Organic Soils* – Various peats and mucks are easily recognized as hydric soils. Organic soils that are cropped are often drained, yet the water table is closely managed to minimize oxidation of organic matter. These soils often retain their hydric soil characteristics and, if so, meet the wetland hydrology criterion.

2) *Histic epipedons* – A histic epipedon (organic surface layer) is an 8- to 16-inch organic layer at or near the surface of a hydric mineral soil that is saturated with water for 30 consecutive days or more in most years. It contains a minimum of 20 percent organic matter when no clay is present or a

minimum of 30 percent organic matter when clay content is 60 percent or greater. Soils with histic epipedons are inundated or saturated for sufficient periods to greatly retard aerobic decomposition of organic matter, and are considered hydric soils. In general, a histic epipedon is a thin surface layer of peat or muck if the soil has not been plowed (U.S.D.A. Soil Survey Staff 1975). Histic epipedons are technically classified as Oa, Oe, or Oi surface layers, and in some cases the terms "mucky" or "peaty" are used as modifiers to the mineral soil texture term, e.g., mucky loam.

3) *Sulfidic material* – When soils emit an odor of rotten eggs, hydrogen sulfide is present. Such odors are only detected in waterlogged soils that are essentially permanently saturated and have sulfidic material within a few inches of the soil surface. Sulfides are produced only in reducing environment. Under saturated conditions, the sulfates in water are biologically reduced to sulfides as the organic materials accumulate.

4) *Aquic or peraquic moisture regime* – An *aquic* moisture regime is a reducing one, i.e., it is virtually free of dissolved oxygen, because the soil is saturated by ground water or by water of the capillary fringe (U.S.D.A. Soil Survey Staff 1975). The soil is considered saturated if water stands in an unlined borehole at a shallow enough depth that the capillary fringe reaches the soil surface, except in noncapillary pores. Because dissolved oxygen is removed from ground water by respiration of microorganisms, roots, and soil fauna, it is also implicit that the soil temperature be above biologic zero (41°F) at some time while the soil is saturated. Soils with *peraquic* moisture regimes are characterized by the presence of ground water always at or near the soil surface. Examples include soils of tidal marshes and soils of closed, landlocked depressions that are fed by permanent streams. Soils with peraquic moisture regimes are always hydric under natural conditions. Soils with aquic moisture regimes are usually hydric, but the NTCHS hydric soil criteria should be verified in the field.

5) *Direct observations of reducing soil conditions* – Soils saturated for long or very long duration will usually exhibit reducing conditions at the time of saturation. Under such conditions, ions of iron are transformed from a ferric (oxidized) state to a ferrous (reduced) state. This reduced condition can often be detected in the field by use of a colorimetric field test kit. When a soil extract changes to a pink color upon addition of a-a-dipyridil, ferrous iron is present, which indicates a reducing soil environment at the time of the test. A negative result (no pink color) only indicates that the soil is not reduced at this moment; it does not imply that the soil is not reduced during the growing season. Furthermore, the test is subject to error due to the rapid change of ferrous iron to ferric iron when the soil is exposed to air and should only be used by experienced technicians. (*CAUTION*: This test cannot be used in hydric mineral soils having low iron content or in organic soils. Also it does not determine the duration of reduced conditions.)

6) *Gleyed, low chroma, and low chroma/ mottled soils* – The colors of various soil components are often the most diagnostic indicator of hydric soils. Colors of these components are strongly influenced by the frequency and duration of soil saturation which leads to reducing soil conditions. Hydric mineral soils will be either gleyed or will have low chroma matrix with or without bright mottles.

A) *Gleyed soils* – Gleying (bluish, greenish, or grayish colors) immediately below the A-horizon is an indication of a markedly reduced soil, and gleyed soils are hydric soils. Gleying can occur in both mottled and unmottled soils. Gleyed soil conditions can be determined by using the gley page of the "Munsell Soil Color Charts" (Kollmorgen Corporation 1975). (*CAUTION*: Gleyed conditions normally extend throughout saturated soils. Beware of soils with gray E-horizons due to leaching and not to saturation; these latter soils can often be recognized by bright-colored layers below the E-horizon.)

B) *Other low chroma soils and mottled soils (i.e., soils with low matrix chroma and with or without bright mottles)* – Hydric mineral soils that are saturated for substantial periods of the growing season, but are unsaturated for some time, commonly develop mottles. Soils that have brightly colored mottles and a low chroma matrix are indicative of a fluctuating water table. Hydric mineral soils usually have one of the following color features in the horizon immediately below the A-horizon:

(1) Matrix chroma of 2 or less in mottled soils, or
(2) Matrix chroma of 1 or less in unmottled soils.

(*Note*: See p. 59 for mollisols exception.)

Colors should be determined in soils that are or have been moistened. The chroma requirements above are for soils in a moistened condition. Colors noted for dry (unmoistened) soils should be clearly stated as such. The colors of the topsoil are often not indicative of the hydrologic situation because cultivation and soil enrichment affect the original soil color. Hence, the soil colors below the A-horizon (usually below 10 inches) often must be examined.

(*CAUTION*: Beware of problematic hydric soils that have colors other than those described above; see problem area wetlands section, p. 55.)

7) *Iron and manganese concretions* – During the oxidation-reduction process, iron and manganese in suspension are sometimes segregated as oxides into concretions or soft masses. Concretions are local concentrations of chemical compounds (e.g., iron oxide) in the form of a grain or nodule of varying size, shape, hardness, and color (Buckman and Brady 1969). Manganese concretions are usually black or dark brown, while iron concretions are usually yellow, orange or reddish brown. In hydric soils, these concretions are also usually accompanied by soil colors described above.

8) *Coarse-textured or sandy hydric soils* – Many of the indicators listed above cannot be applied to sandy soils. *In particular, soil color should not be used as an indicator in most sandy soils* (see problem area wetlands section, p. 55). However, three soil features may be used as indicators of hydric sandy soils:

A) *High organic matter content in the surface horizon* – Organic matter tends to accumulate above or in the surface horizon of sandy soils that are inundated or saturated to the surface for a significant portion of the growing season. The mineral surface layer generally appears darker than the mineral material immediately below it due to organic matter interspersed among or adhering to sand particles. (*Note*: Because organic matter also accumulates on upland soils, in some instances it may be difficult to distinguish a surface organic layer associated with a wetland site from litter and duff associated with an upland site unless the species composition of the organic materials is determined.)

B) *Dark vertical streaking of subsurface horizons by organic matter* – Organic matter is moved downward through sand as the water table fluctuates. This often occurs more rapidly and to a greater degree in some vertical sections of a sandy soil containing high content of organic matter than in others. Thus, the sandy soil appears vertically streaked with darker areas. When soil from a darker area is rubbed between the fingers, the dark organic matter stains the fingers.

C) *Wet Spodosols* – As organic matter is moved downward through some sandy soils, it may accumulate at the point representing the most commonly occurring depth to the water table. This organic matter may become slightly cemented with aluminum. Spodic horizons often occur at depths of 12 to 30 inches below the mineral surface. Wet spodosols (formerly called "groundwater podzolic soils") usually have thick dark surface horizons that are high in organic matter with thick, dull gray E-horizons above a very dark-colored (black) spodic horizon. (*CAUTION*: Not all soils with spodic horizons meet the hydric soil criterion; see p. 58.)

(*Note*: In recently deposited sandy material, such as accreting sand bars, it may be impossible to find any of the above indicators. Such cases are considered natural, problem area wetlands and the determination of hydric soil should be based on knowledge of local hydrology. See p. 57-58).

Wetland Hydrology

3.29. The driving force creating wetlands is "wetland hydrology", that is, permanent or periodic inundation, or soil saturation for a significant period (usually a week or more) during the growing season. All wetlands are, therefore, at least periodically wet. Many wetlands are found along rivers, lakes, and estuaries where flooding is likely to occur, while other wetlands form in isolated depressions surrounded by upland where surface water collects. Still others develop on slopes of varying steepness, in surface water drainageways or where ground water discharges to the land surface in spring or seepage areas.

3.30. Numerous factors influence the wetness of an area, including precipitation, stratigraphy, topography, soil permeability, and plant cover. The frequency and duration of inundation or soil saturation are important in separating wetlands from non-wetlands. Duration usually is the more important factor. Areas of lower elevation in a floodplain or marsh have longer duration of inundation and saturation and often more frequent periods of these conditions than most areas at higher levels. Floodplain configuration may significantly affect the duration of inundation by facilitating rapid runoff or by causing poor drainage. Soil permeability related to the texture of the soil also influences the duration of inundation or soil saturation. For example, clayey soils absorb water more slowly than sandy or loamy soils, and therefore have slower permeability and remain saturated much longer. Type and amount of plant cover affect both degree of inundation and duration of saturated soil conditions. Excess water drains more slowly in areas of abundant plant cover, thereby increasing duration of inundation or soil saturation. On the other hand, transpiration rates are higher in areas of abundant plant cover, which may reduce the duration of soil saturation.

3.31. To determine whether the wetland hydrology criterion is met, one should consider recorded data, aerial photographs, and field indicators that provide direct or indirect evidence of inundation or soil saturation.

Recorded Data

3.32. Recorded hydrologic data usually provides both short- and long-term information on the frequency and duration of flooding, but little or no information on soil saturation periods. Recorded data include stream gauge data, lake gauge data, tidal gauge data, flood predictions, and historical flood records. Use of these data is commonly limited to areas adjacent to streams and other similar areas. Recorded data may be available from the following sources:

1) CE district offices (data for major waterbodies and for site-specific areas from planning and design documents)

2) U.S. Geological Survey (stream and tidal gauge data)

3) National Oceanic and Atmospheric Administration (tidal gauge data)

4) State, county and local agencies (flood data)

5) SCS state offices (small watershed projects data)

6) private developers or landowners (site-specific hydrologic data, which may include water table or groundwater well data).

Aerial Photographs

3.33. Aerial photographs may provide direct evidence of inundation or soil saturation in an area. Inundation (flooding or ponding) is best observed during the early spring in temperate and boreal regions when snow and ice are gone and leaves of deciduous trees and shrubs are not yet present. This allows detection of wet soil conditions that would be obscured by the tree or shrub canopy at full leaf-out. For marshes, this season of photography is also desirable, except in regions characterized by distinct dry and rainy seasons, such as southern Florida and California. Wetland hydrology would be best observed during the wet season in these latter areas.

3.34. It is most desirable to examine several consecutive years of early spring or wet season aerial photographs to document evidence of wetland inundation or soil saturation. In this way, the effects of abnormally dry springs, for example, may be minimized. In interpreting aerial photographs, it is important to know the antecedent weather conditions. This will help eliminate potential misinterpretations caused by abnormally wet or dry periods. Contact the U.S. Weather Service for historical weather records. Aerial photographs for agricultural regions of the country are often available at county offices of the Agricultural Stabilization and Conservation Service.

Field Indicators

3.35. At certain times of the year in most wetlands, and in certain types of wetlands at most times, wetland hydrology is quite evident, since surface water or saturated soils (e.g., soggy or wetter underfoot) may be observed. Yet in many instances, especially along the uppermost boundary of wetlands, hydrology is not readily apparent. Consequently, the wetland hydrology criterion is often impracticable for delineating precise wetland boundaries. Despite this limitation, hydrologic indicators can be useful for confirming that a site with hydrophytic vegetation and hydric soils still exhibits wetland hydrology and that the hydrology has not been significantly modified to the extent that the area is now effectively drained. In other words, while hydrologic indicators are sometimes diagnostic of the presence of wetlands, they are generally either operationally impracticable (e.g., in the case of recorded data) or technically inaccurate (e.g., in the case of some field indicators) for delineating wetland boundaries. In the former case, surveying the wetland boundary according to elevation data related to recorded flood data, for example, is generally too time-consuming and may not actually be a true correlation. In the latter case, it should be quite obvious that indicators of flooding often extend well beyond the wetland boundary into low-lying upland areas that were flooded by an infrequent flood. Consequently the emphasis on delineating wetland boundaries should be placed on hydrophytic vegetation and hydric soils in the absence of significant hydrologic modification, although wetland hydrology should always be considered.

3.36. If significant drainage or groundwater alteration has taken place, then it is necessary to determine whether the area in question is effectively drained and is now nonwetland or is only partly drained and remains wetland despite some hydrologic modification. Guidance for determining whether an area is effectively drained is presented in the section on disturbed areas (p. 50). In the absence of visible evidence of significant hydrologic modification, wetland hydrology is presumed to occur in an area having hydrophytic vegetation and hydric soils.

3.37. The following hydrologic indicators can be assessed quickly in the field. Although some are not necessarily indicative of hydrologic events during the growing season or in wetlands alone, they do provide evidence that inundation or soil saturation have occurred at some time. One should use good professional judgement in deciding whether the hydrologic indicators demonstrate that the wetland hydrology criterion has been satisfied. When considering these indicators, it is important to be aware of recent extreme flooding events and heavy rainfall periods that could cause low-lying nonwetlands to exhibit some of these signs. It is, therefore, best to avoid, if possible, field inspections

during and immediately after these events. If not possible, then these events must be considered in making a wetland determination. Also, remember that hydrology varies seasonally and annually as well as daily, and that at significant times of the year (e.g., late summer for most of the country) the water tables are at their lowest points. At these low water periods, signs of soil saturation and flooding may be difficult to find in many wetlands.

1) *Visual observation of inundation* – The most obvious and revealing hydrologic indicator may be simply observing the areal extent of inundation. However, both seasonal conditions and recent weather conditions should be considered when observing an area because they can affect whether surface water is present on a nonwetland site.

2) *Visual observation of soil saturation* – In some cases, saturated soils are obvious, since the ground surface is soggy or mucky under foot. In many cases, however, examination of this indicator requires digging a hole to a depth of 18 inches and observing the level at which water stands in the hole after sufficient time has been allowed for water to drain into the hole. The required time will vary depending on soil texture. In some cases, the upper level at which water is flowing into the hole can be observed by examining the wall of the hole. This level represents the depth to the water table. The depth to saturated soils will always be nearer the surface due to a capillary fringe. In some heavy clay soils, water may not rapidly accumulate in the hole even when the soil is saturated. If water is observed at the bottom of the hole but has not filled to the 12-inch depth, examine the sides of the hole and determine the shallowest depth at which water is entering the hole. Saturated soils may also be detected by a "squeeze test," which involves taking a soil sample within 18 inches (actual depth depends on soil permeability) and squeezing the sample. If free water can be extracted, the soil is saturated at the depth of the sample at this point in time. When applying the soil saturation indicator, both the season of the year and the preceding weather conditions must be considered. (*Note*: It is not necessary to directly demonstrate soil saturation at the time of inspection. If the NTCHS criteria for hydric soil are met, it can be assumed that an area is saturated to the surface or inundated at some point in time during an average rainfall year.)

3) *Oxidized channels (rhizospheres) associated with living roots and rhizomes* – Some plants are

able to survive saturated soil conditions (i.e., a reducing environment) because they can transport oxygen to their root zone. Look for iron oxide concretions (orangish or reddish brown in color) forming along the channels of living roots and rhizomes as evidence of soil saturation (anaerobic conditions) for a significant period during the growing season.

4) *Water marks* – Water marks are found most commonly on woody vegetation but may also be observed on other vegetation. They often occur as stains on bark or other fixed objects (e.g., bridge pillars, buildings, and fences). When several water marks are present, the highest usually reflects the maximum extent of recent inundation.

5) *Drift lines* – This indicator is typically found adjacent to streams or other sources of water flow in wetlands and often occurs in tidal marshes. Evidence consists of deposition of debris in a line on the wetland surface or debris entangled in above-ground vegetation or other fixed objects. Debris usually consists of remnants of vegetation (branches, stems, and leaves), sediment, litter, and other water-borne materials deposited more or less parallel to the direction of water flow. Drift lines provide an indication of the minimum portion of the area inundated during a flooding event; the maximum level of inundation is generally at a higher elevation than that indicated by a drift line.

6) *Water-borne sediment deposits* – Plants and other vertical objects often have thin layers, coatings, or depositions of mineral or organic matter on them after inundation. This evidence may remain for a considerable period before it is removed by precipitation or subsequent inundation. Sediment deposition on vegetation and other objects provides an indication of the minimum inundation level. When sediments are primarily organic (e.g., fine organic material and algae), the detritus may become encrusted on or slightly above the soil surface after dewatering occurs.

7) *Water-stained leaves* – Forested wetlands that are inundated earlier in the year will frequently have water-stained leaves on the forest floor. These leaves are generally grayish or blackish in appearance, darkened from being underwater for significant periods.

8) *Surface scoured areas* – Surface scouring occurs along floodplains where overbank flooding erodes sediments (e.g., at the bases of trees). The

absence of leaf litter from the soil surface is also sometimes an indication of surface scouring. Forested wetlands that contain standing waters for relatively long duration will occasionally have areas of bare or essentially bare soil, sometimes associated with local depressions.

9) *Wetland drainage patterns* – Many wetlands (e.g., tidal marshes and floodplain wetlands) have characteristic meandering or braided drainage patterns that are readily recognized in the field or on aerial photographs and occasionally on topographic maps. (*CAUTION*: Drainage patterns also occur in upland areas after periods of considerable precipitation; therefore, topographic position also must be considered when applying this indicator.)

10) *Morphological plant adaptations* – Many plants growing in wetlands have developed morphological adaptations in response to inundation or soil saturation. Examples include pneumatophores, buttressed tree trunks, multiple trunks, adventitious roots, shallow root systems, floating stems, floating leaves, polymorphic leaves, hypertrophied lenticels, inflated leaves, stems or roots, and aerenchyma (air-filled) tissue in roots and stems (see Table 1 for examples). As long as there is no evidence of significant hydrologic modification, these adaptations can be used as hydrologic indicators. Moreover, when these features are observed in young plants, they provide good evidence that recent wetland hydrology exists. (*Note*: While some people may consider these morphological adaptations as indicators of hydrophytic vegetation, for purposes of this manual, they are treated as indicators of wetland hydrology because they typically develop in response to permanent or periodic inundation or soil saturation.)

11) *Hydric soil characteristics* – In the absence of the above indicators, if an area meets the field indicators for hydric soils and there is no indication of significant hydrologic modification, then it can be assumed that the area meets the wetland hydrology criterion. If the area has been significantly disturbed hydrologically, refer to the section on disturbed areas (p. 50). (*CAUTION*: Listing of a soil on the NTCHS list of hydric soils does not necessarily mean the wetland hydrology criterion is met, nor does exclusion of a soil from the list demonstrate that the wetland hydrology criterion has not been met. However, soils on the NTCHS list represent those soils which typically meet the wetland hydrology criterion, unless effectively drained or otherwise altered.)

Table 1. Morphological or structural adaptations of plants for growing in permanently or periodically flooded or saturated soils.

Adaptations	Examples of Plants Possessing Adaptation
Buttressed (swollen) Tree Trunk	Bald Cypress (*Taxodium distichum*), Black Gum (*Nyssa sylvatica* var. *biflora*), Green Ash (*Fraxinus pennsylvanica* var. *subintegerima*), Water Gum (*Nyssa aquatica*), and Ogechee Tupelo (*Nyssa ogechee*)
Multiple Trunks	Red Maple (*Acer rubrum*), Silver maple (*Acer saccharinum*), Swamp Privet (*Forestiera acuminata*), and Ogechee Tupelo
Pneumataphores	Bald Cypress, Water Gum, and Black Mangrove (*Rhizophora mangle*)
Adventitious Roots (arising from stem above ground)	Box Elder (*Acer negundo*), Sycamore (*Platanus occidentalis*), Pin Oak (*Quercus palustris*), Black Willow (*Salix nigra*), Green Ash, Alligatorweed (*Alternanthera philoxeroides*), Water Primroses (*Ludwigia* spp.), Water Gum, Eastern Cottonwood (*Populus deltoides*), and Willows (*Salix* spp.)
Shallow Roots (often exposed to ground surface)	Red Maple and Laurel Oak (*Quercus laurifolia*)
Hypertrophied Lenticels	Red Maple, Silver Maple, Willows, Black Mangrove, Water Locust (*Gleditsia aquatica*), and Sweet Gale (*Myrica gale*)
Aerenchyma (air-filled tissue) in Roots & Stems	Eastern Bur-reed (*Sparganium americanum*), Soft Rush (*Juncus effusus*), Soft-stemmed Bulrush (*Scirpus validus*), Water Shield (*Brasenia schreberi*), Umbrella Sedges (*Cyperus* spp.), other Rushes (*Juncus* spp.), Spike-rushes (*Eleocharis* spp.), Twig-rush (*Cladium mariscoides*), Buckbean (*Menyanthes trifoliata*), Giant Bur-reed (*Sparganium eurycarpum*), and Cattails (*Typha* spp.)
Polymorphic Leaves	Arrowheads (*Sagittaria* spp.) and Water Parsnip (*Sium suave*)
Floating Leaves	Water Shield, Spatterdock Lily (*Nuphar luteum*), and White Water Lily (*Nymphaea odorata*)

Sources: Environmental Laboratory (1987) and Tiner (1988).

Part IV.
Methods for Identification and Delineation of Wetlands

4.0. Four basic approaches for identifying and delineating wetlands have been developed to cover situations ranging from desk-top or office determinations to highly complex field determinations for regulatory purposes. These methods are the recommended approaches and the reasons for departing from them should be documented. Remember, however, that any method for making a wetland determination must consider the three technical criteria (i.e., hydrophytic vegetation, hydric soils, and wetland hydrology) listed in Part II of this manual. These criteria must be met in order to identify a wetland. In applying all methods, relevant available information on wetlands in the area of concern should be collected and reviewed. Table 2 lists primary data sources.

Selection of a Method

4.1. The wetland delineation methods presented in this manual can be grouped into two general types: (1) offsite procedures and (2) onsite procedures. The offsite procedures are designed for use in the office, while onsite procedures are developed for use in the field. When an onsite inspection is unnecessary or cannot be undertaken for various reasons, available information can be reviewed in the office to make a wetland determination. If available information is insufficient to make a wetland determination or if a precise wetland boundary must be established, an onsite inspection should be conducted. Depending on the field information needed or the complexity of the area, one of three basic onsite methods may be employed: (1) routine, (2) intermediate-level, or (3) comprehensive.

4.2. The routine method is designed for areas equal to or less than five acres in size or larger areas with homogeneous vegetation. For areas greater than five acres in size or other areas of any size that are highly diverse in vegetation, the intermediate-level method or the comprehensive method should be applied, as necessary. The comprehensive method is applied to situations requiring detailed documentation of vegetation, soils, and hydrology. Assessments of significantly disturbed sites will often require intermediate-level or comprehensive determinations as well as some special procedures. In other cases where natural conditions make wetland identification difficult, special procedures for problem area wetland determinations have been developed. These procedures are subroutines of the three onsite determination methods. In making wetland determinations, one should select the appropriate method for each individual unit within the area of concern and not necessarily employ one method for the entire site. Thus, a combination of determination methods may be used for a given site.

4.3. Regardless of the method used, the desired outcome or final product is a wetland/nonwetland determination. Depending on one's expertise, available information, and individual or agency preference, there are two basic approaches to delineating wetland boundaries. The first approach involves characterizing plant communities in the area, identifying hydrophytic plant communities, examining the soils in these areas to confirm the presence of hydric soil, and finally looking for evidence of wetland hydrology. This approach has been widely used by the CE and EPA and to a large extent by the FWS. A second approach involves first delineating the boundary of hydric soils, and then verifying the presence of hydrophytic vegetation and looking for signs of wetland hydrology. This type of approach has been employed by the SCS and to a limited extent by the FWS. Since these approaches yield the same result, this manual incorporates both approaches into most of the methods presented.

Table 2. Primary sources of information that may be helpful in making a wetland determination.

Data Name	Source
Topographic Maps (mostly 1:24,000; 1:63,350 for Alaska)	U.S. Geological Survey (USGS) (Call 1-800-USA-MAPS)
National Wetlands Inventory Maps (mostly 1:24,000; 1:63,350 for Alaska)	U.S. Fish and Wildlife Service (FWS) (Call 1-800-USA-MAPS)
County Soil Survey Reports	U.S.D.A. Soil Conservation Service (SCS) District Offices (Unpublished reports--local district offices)
National Hydric Soils List	SCS National Office
State Hydric Soils List	SCS State Offices
County Hydric Soil Map Unit List	SCS District Offices
National Insurance Agency Flood Maps	Federal Emergency Management Agency
Local Wetland Maps	State and local agencies
Land Use and Land Cover Maps	USGS (1-800-USA-MAPS)
Aerial Photographs	Various sources--USGS, U.S.D.A. Agricultural Stabilization and Conservation Service, other Federal and State agencies, and private sources
Satellite Imagery	EOSAT Corporation, SPOT Corporation, and others
National List of Plant Species That Occur in Wetlands (Stock No. 024-010-00682-0)	Government Printing Office Superintendent of Documents Washington, DC 20402
Regional Lists of Plants that Occur in Wetlands	National Technical Information Service 5285 Port Royal Head Springfield, VA 22161 (703) 487-4650
National Wetland Plant Database	FWS
Stream Gauge Data	CE District Offices and USGS
Soil Drainage Guides	SCS District Offices
Environmental Impact Statements and Assessments	Various Federal and State agencies
Published Reports	Federal and States agencies, universities, and others
Local Expertise	Universities, consultants, and others
Site-specific Plans and Engineering Designs	Private developers

Description of Methods

Offsite Determinations

4.4. When an onsite inspection is not necessary because information on hydrology, hydric soils, and hydrophytic vegetation is known or an inspection is not possible due to time constraints or other reasons, a wetland determination can be made in the office. This approach provides a best approximation of the presence of wetland and its boundaries based on available information. The accuracy of the determination depends on the quality of the information used and on one's ability and experience in an area to interpret these data. Where reliable, site-specific data have been previously collected, the wetland determination should be reasonably accurate. Where these data do not exist, more generalized information may be used to make a preliminary wetland determination. In either case, however, if a more accurate delineation is required, then onsite procedures must be employed.

Offsite Determination Method

4.5. The following steps are recommended for conducting an offsite wetland determination:

Step 1. *Locate the area of interest on a U.S.Geological Survey topographic map and delineate the approximate subject area boundary on the map.* Note whether marsh or swamp symbols or lakes, ponds, rivers, and other waterbodies are present within the area. If they are, then there is a good likelihood that wetland is present. Proceed to Step 2.

Step 2. *Review appropriate National Wetlands Inventory (NWI) maps, State wetland maps, or local wetland maps, where available.* If these maps designate wetlands in the subject area, there is a high probability that wetlands are present unless there is evidence on hand that the wetlands have been effectively drained, filled, excavated, impounded, or otherwise significantly altered since the effective date of the maps. Proceed to Step 3.

Step 3. *Review SCS soil survey maps where available.* In the area of interest, are there any map units listed on the county list of hydric soil map units or are there any soil map units with significant hydric soil inclusions? If *YES*, then assume that at least a portion of the project area

may be wetland. If this area is also shown as a wetland on NWI or other wetland maps, then there is a high probability that the area is wetland unless it has been recently altered (check recent aerial photos, Step 4). Areas without hydric soils or hydric soil inclusions should in most cases be eliminated from further review, but aerial photos still should be examined for small wetlands to be more certain. This is especially true if wetlands have been designated on the National Wetlands Inventory or other wetland maps. Proceed to Step 4.

Step 4. *Review recent aerial photos of the project area.* Before reviewing aerial photos, evaluate climatological data to determine whether the photo year had normal or abnormal (high or low) precipitation two to three months, for example, prior to the date of the photo. This will help provide a useful perspective or frame-of-reference for doing photo interpretation. In some cases, aerial photos covering a multi-year period (e.g., 5-7 years) should be reviewed, especially where recent climatic conditions have been abnormal.

During photo interpretation, look for one or more signs of wetlands. For example:

> 1) hydrophytic vegetation;
> 2) surface water;
> 3) saturated soils;
> 4) flooded or drowned out crops;
> 5) stressed crops due to wetness;
> 6) greener crops in dry years;
> 7) differences in vegetation patterns due to different planting dates.

If signs of wetland are observed, proceed to Step 5 when site-specific data are available; if site-specific data are not available, proceed to Step 6.

(*CAUTION*: Accurate photo interpretation of certain wetland types requires considerable expertise. Evergreen forested wetlands and temporarily flooded wetlands, in general, may present considerable difficulty. If not proficient in wetland photo interpretation, then one can rely more on the findings of other sources, such as NWI maps and soil surveys, or seek help in photo interpretation.)

Step 5. *Review available site-specific information.* In some cases, information on vegetation, soils, and hydrology for the project area has been collected during previous visits to the area by agency personnel, environmental consultants or others.

Moreover, individuals or experts having firsthand knowledge of the project site should be contacted for information whenever possible. Be sure, however, to know the reliability of these sources. After reviewing this information, proceed to Step 6.

Step 6. *Determine whether wetlands exist in the subject area.* Based on a review of existing information, wetlands can be assumed to exist if:

1) Wetlands are shown on NWI or other wetland maps, and hydric soil or a soil with hydric soil inclusions is shown on the soil survey; or

2) Hydric soil or soil with hydric soil inclusions is shown on the soil survey, and

A) site-specific information confirms hydrophytic vegetation, hydric soils, and/or wetland hydrology, or

B) signs of wetland are detected by reviewing aerial photos; or

3) Any combination of the above or parts thereof (e.g., vegetated wetland on NWI maps and signs of wetland on aerial photos).

If after examining the available reference material one is still unsure whether wetland occurs in the area, then a field inspection should be conducted, whenever possible. Alternatively, more detailed information on the site characteristics may be sought from the project sponsor, if applicable, to help make the determination.

4.6. Offsite procedures are dependent on the availability of information for making a wetland determination, the quality of this information, and one's ability and experience to interpret these data. In most cases, therefore, the offsite procedure yields a preliminary determination. For more accurate results, one must conduct an onsite inspection.

Onsite Determinations

4.7. When an onsite inspection is necessary, be sure to review pertinent background information (e.g., NWI maps, soil surveys, and site plans) before going to the subject site. This information will be helpful in determining what type of field method should be employed. Also, read the sections of this manual that discuss disturbed and problem area wetlands before conducting field work (see p. 50-59). Recommended equipment and materials for conducting onsite determinations are listed in Table 3.

Figures 1, 2, and 3 show the conceptual approaches for making onsite wetland determinations. These figures are *NOT* decision matrices for making wetland determinations.

Table 3. Recommended equipment and materials for onsite determinations.

Equipment	Materials
Soil auger, probe, or spade	Data sheets and clipboard
Sighting compass	Field notebook
Pen or pencil	Base (topographic) map
Penknife	Aerial photograph
Hand lens	National Wetlands Inventory map
Vegetation sampling frame*	Soil survey or other soil map
Camera/Film	Appropriate Federal interagency wetland plants list
Binoculars	County hydric soil map unit list
Tape measure	Munsell scoil color book
Prism or angle gauge	Plant identification field guides/manuals
Diameter tape*	*National List of Scientific Plant Names*
Vasculum (for plant collection)	Flagging tape/wire flags/wooden stakes
Calculator*	Plastic bags (for collecting plants and soil samples as needed)
Dissecting kit	

* Needed for comprehensive determination

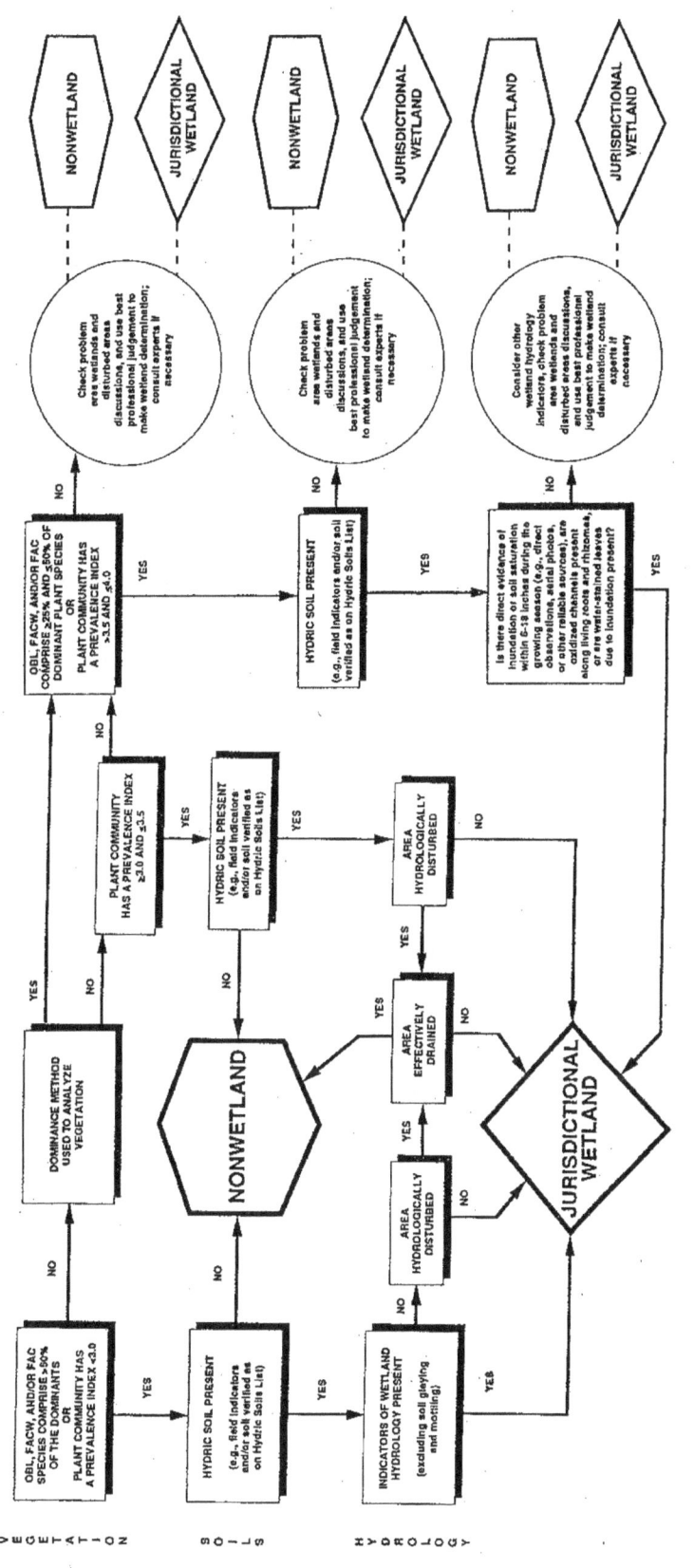

Figure 1. Composite of Conceptual Approaches for Making an Onsite Jurisdictional Wetland Determination. (*CAUTION:* This is NOT a Decision Matrix for Making a Wetland Determination.)

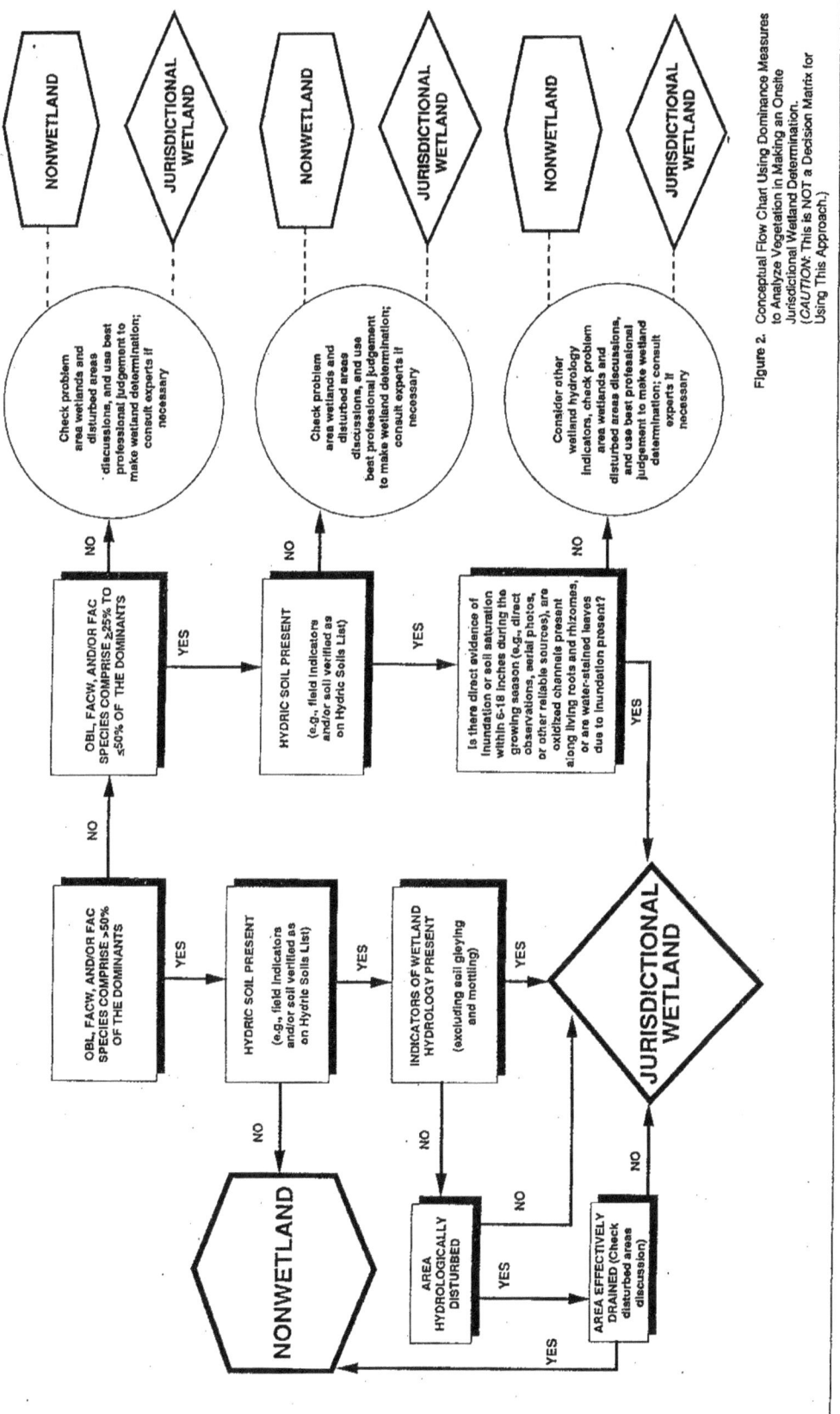

Figure 2. Conceptual Flow Chart Using Dominance Measures to Analyze Vegetation in Making an Onsite Jurisdictional Wetland Determination. (*CAUTION:* This is NOT a Decision Matrix for Using This Approach.)

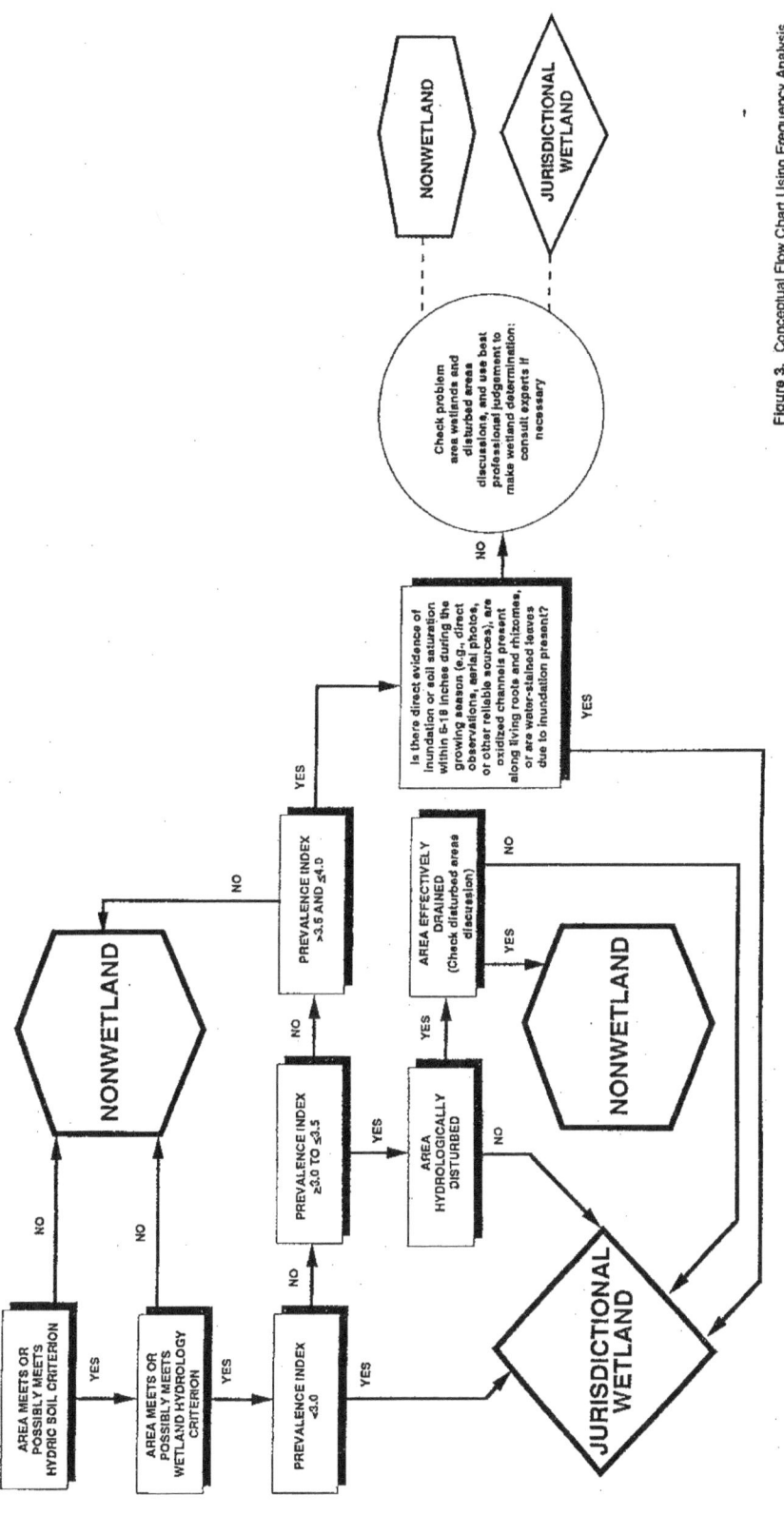

Figure 3. Conceptual Flow Chart Using Frequency Analysis (Point Intercept Sampling Procedures) of Vegetation in Making an Onsite Jurisdictional Determination. (*CAUTION:* This is NOT a Decision Matrix for Making a Wetland Determination.)

4.8. For every upcoming field inspection, the following pre-inspection steps should be undertaken:

Step 1. *Locate the project area on a map (e.g., U.S. Geological Survey topographic map or SCS soil survey map) or on an aerial photograph and determine the limits of the area of concern.* Proceed to Step 2.

Step 2. *Estimate the size of the subject area.* Proceed to Step 3.

Step 3. *Review existing background information and determine, to the extent possible, the site's geomorphological setting (e.g., floodplain, isolated depression, or ridge and swale complex), its habitat or vegetative complexity (i.e., the range of habitat or vegetation types), and its soils.* (*Note*: Depending on available information, it may not be possible to determine the habitat complexity without going on the site; if necessary, do a field reconnaissance.) Proceed to Step 4.

Step 4. *Determine whether a disturbed condition exists.* Examine available information and determine whether there is evidence of sufficient natural or human-induced alteration to significantly modify all or a portion of the area's vegetation, soils, and/or hydrology. If such disturbance is noted, identify the limits of affected areas for they should be evaluated separately for wetland determination purposes (usually after evaluating undisturbed areas). The presence of disturbed areas within the subject area should be considered when selecting an onsite determination method. (*Note*: It may be possible that at any time during this determination, one or more of the three characteristics may be found to be significantly altered. If this happens, follow the disturbed area wetland determination procedures, as necessary, noted on p. 50.) Proceed to Step 5.

Step 5. *Determine the field determination method to be used.* Considering the size and complexity of the area, determine whether a routine, intermediate-level, or comprehensive field determination method should be used. When the area is equal to or less than five acres in size or is larger and appears to be relatively homogeneous with respect to vegetation, soils, and/or hydrology, use the routine method (see below). When the area is greater than five acres in size, or is smaller but appears to be highly diverse with respect to vegetation, use the intermediate-level method (p. 35).

When detailed quantification of plant communities and more extensive documentation of other factors (soils and hydrology) are required, use the comprehensive method regardless of the wetland's size (p. 39.) Significantly disturbed sites (e.g., sites that have been filled, hydrologically modified, cleared of vegetation, or had their soils altered) will generally require intermediate-level or comprehensive methods. In these disturbed areas, it usually will be necessary to follow a set of subroutines to determine whether the altered characteristic met the applicable criterion prior to its modification; in the case of altered wetland hydrology, it may be necessary to determine whether the area is effectively drained. Because a large area may include a diversity of smaller areas ranging from simple wetlands to vegetatively complex areas, one may use a combination of the onsite determination methods, as appropriate.

Routine Onsite Determination Method

4.9. For most cases, wetland determinations can be made in the field without rigorous sampling of vegetation and soils. Two approaches for routine determinations are presented: (1) hydric soil assessment procedure, and (2) plant community assessment procedure. In the former approach, areas that meet or may meet the hydric soil criterion are first delineated and then dominant vegetation is visually estimated to determine if hydrophytic vegetation is obvious. If so, the area is designated as wetland. If not, then the site must undergo a more rigorous evaluation following one of the other onsite determination methods presented in the manual. The second routine approach requires initial identification of representative plant community types in the subject area and then characterization of vegetation, soils, and hydrology for each type. After identifying wetland and nonwetland communities, the wetland boundary is delineated. All pertinent observations on the three mandatory wetland criteria should be recorded on an appropriate data sheet.

4.10. Hydric Soil Assessment Procedure

Step 1. *Identify the approximate limits of areas that may meet the hydric soil criterion within the area of concern and sketch limits on an aerial photograph.* To help identify these limits use sources of information such as Agricultural Stabilization and Conservation slides, soil surveys, NWI maps, and other maps and photographs. (*Note*: This step is more convenient to perform offsite, but may be done onsite.) Proceed to Step 2.

Step 2. *Scan the areas that may meet the hydric soil criterion and determine if disturbed conditions exist.* Are any significantly disturbed areas present? If *YES*, identify their limits for they should be evaluated separately for wetland determination purposes (usually after evaluating undisturbed areas). Refer to the section on disturbed areas (p. 50), if necessary, to evaluate the altered characteristic(s) (vegetation, soils, or hydrology); then return to this method and continue evaluating characteristics not altered. (*Note*: Prior experience with disturbed sites may allow one to easily evaluate an altered characteristic, such as when vegetation is not present in a farmed wetland due to cultivation.) Keep in mind that if at any time during this determination, one or more of these three characteristics are found to have been significantly altered, the disturbed area determination procedures should be followed. If the area is not significantly disturbed, proceed to Step 3.

Step 3. *Scan the areas that may meet the hydric soil criterion and determine if obvious signs of wetland hydrology are present.* The wetland hydrology criterion is met for any area or portion thereof where it is obvious or known that the area is frequently inundated or saturated to the surface during the growing season. If the above condition exists, the hydric soil criterion is met for the subject area and the area is considered wetland. If necessary, confirm the presence of hydric soil by examining the soil for appropriate field indicators. (*Note*: Hydrophytic vegetation is assumed to be present under these conditions, i.e., undrained hydric soil, so vegetation does not need to be examined. Moreover, hydrophytic vegetation should be obvious in these situations.) Areas lacking obvious indicators of wetland hydrology must be further examined, so proceed to Step 4.

Step 4. *Refine the boundary of areas that meet the hydric soil criterion.* Verify the presence of hydric soil within the appropriate map units by digging a number of holes at least 18 inches deep along the boundary (interface) between hydric soil units and nonhydric soil units. Compare soil samples with descriptions in the soil survey report to see if they are properly mapped and look for hydric

soil characteristics or indicators. In this way, the boundary of areas meeting the hydric soil criterion is further refined by field observations. In map units where only part of the unit is hydric (e.g., complexes, associations, and inclusions), locate hydric soil areas on the ground by considering landscape position and evaluating soil characteristics for hydric soil properties (indicators). (*Note*: Some hydric soils, especially organic soils, have not been given a series name and are referred to by common names, such as peat, muck, swamp, marsh, wet alluvial land, tidal marsh, sulfaquents, and sulfihemists. These areas are also considered hydric soil map units. Certain hydric soils are mapped with nonhydric soils as an association or complex, while other hydric soils occur as inclusions in nonhydric map units. Only the hydric soil portion of these map units should be evaluated for hydrophytic vegetation in Step 7.) If the area meets the hydric soil criterion, proceed to Step 5. (*Note*: These areas are also considered to have met the wetland hydrology criterion.)

Step 5. *Determine whether normal environmental conditions are present.* Determine whether normal environmental conditions are present by considering the following:

1) Is the area presently lacking hydrophytic vegetation or hydrologic indicators due to annual, seasonal or longterm fluctuations in precipitation, surface water, or ground-water levels?

2) Are hydrophytic vegetation indicators lacking due to seasonal fluctuation in temperature (e.g., seasonality of plant growth)?

If the answer to either of these questions is *YES* or uncertain, proceed to the section on problem area wetland determinations (p. 55). If the answer to both questions is *NO*, normal conditions are assumed to be present, so proceed to Step 6.

Step 6. *Select representative observation area(s).* Identify one or more observation areas that represent the area(s) meeting the hydric soil criterion. A representative observation area is one in which the apparent characteristics (determined visually) best represent characteristics of the entire community. Mark the approximate location of the observation area(s) on the aerial photo. Proceed to Step 7.

Step 7. *Characterize the plant community within the area(s) meeting the hydric soil criterion.* Visually estimate the percent areal cover of dominant species for the entire plant community. (*Note:* Dominant species are the most abundant species in each stratum, see p. 9.) If dominant species are not obvious, use one of the other onsite methods. Proceed to Step 8 or to another method, as appropriate.

Step 8. *Record the indicator status of dominant species within each area meeting the hydric soil criterion.* Indicator status is obtained from the interagency Federal list of plants occurring in wetlands for the appropriate geographic region. Record information on an appropriate data form. Proceed to Step 9.

Step 9. *Determine whether wetland is present or additional analysis is required.* If the estimated percent areal cover of OBL and FACW species exceeds that of FACU and UPL species, the area is considered wetland and the wetland-nonwetland boundary is the line delineated in Step 3. If not, then the point intercept or other sampling procedures should be performed to do a more rigorous analysis of site characteristics.

4.11. Plant Community Assessment Procedure

Step 1. *Scan the entire project area, if possible, or walk, if necessary, and identify plant community types present.* In identifying communities, pay particular attention to changes in elevation throughout the site. (*CAUTION:* In highly variable sites, such as ridge and swale complexes, be sure to stratify properly.) If possible, sketch the approximate location of each plant community on a base map, an aerial photograph of the project area, or a county soil survey map and label each community with an appropriate name. (*Note:* For large homogeneous wetlands, especially marshes dominated by herbaceous plants and shrub bogs dominated by low-growing shrubs, it is usually not necessary to walk the entire project area. In these cases, one can often see for long distances and many have organic mucky soils that can be extremely difficult to walk on. Forested areas, however, will usually require a walk through the entire project area.)

In examining the project area, are any significantly disturbed areas observed? If *YES*, identify their limits for they should be evaluated separately for wetland determination purpose (usually after evaluating undisturbed areas). Refer to the section on disturbed areas (p. 50) to evaluate the altered characteristic(s) (i.e., vegetation, soils, or hydrology); then return to this method to continue evaluating characteristics not altered. Keep in mind that if at any time during this determination one or more of these three characteristics are found to have been significantly altered, the disturbed area procedures should be followed. If the area is not significantly disturbed, proceed to Step 2.

Step 2. *Determine whether normal environmental conditions are present.* Determine whether normal environmental conditions are present for each plant community by considering the following:

1) Is the area presently lacking hydrophytic vegetation or hydrologic indicators due to annual, seasonal or long-term fluctuations in precipitation, surface water, or ground-water levels?

2) Are hydrophytic vegetation indicators lacking due to seasonal fluctuations in temperature (e.g., seasonality of plant growth)?

If the answer to either of these questions is *YES* or uncertain, proceed to the section on problem area wetland determinations (p. 55). If the answer to both questions is *NO*, normal conditions are assumed to be present, so proceed to Step 3.

Step 3. *Select representative observation area(s).* Select one or more representative observation areas within each community type. A representative observation area is one in which the apparent characteristics (determined visually) best represent characteristics of the entire community. Mark the approximate location of the observation areas on the base map or photo. Proceed to Step 4.

Step 4. *Characterize each plant community in the project area.* Within each plant community identified in Step 1, visually estimate the dominant plant species for each vegetative stratum in the representative observation areas and record them on an appropriate data form. Vegetative strata may include tree, sapling, shrub, herb, woody vine, and bryophyte strata (see glossary for definitions). A separate form must be completed for each plant community identified for wetland determination purposes. (*Note*: Dominant species are those species in each stratum that, when ranked in decreasing order of abundance and cumulatively totaled, immediately exceed 50 percent of the total dominance measure for that stratum, plus any additional plant species comprising 20 percent or more of the total dominance measure for the stratum.) After identifying dominants within each vegetative stratum, proceed to Step 5.

Step 5. *Record the indicator status of dominant species in all strata.* Indicator status is obtained from the interagency Federal list of plants occurring in wetlands for the appropriate geographic region. Record indicator status for all dominant plant species on a data form. Proceed to Step 6.

Step 6. *Determine whether the hydrophytic vegetation criterion is met.* When more than 50 percent of the dominant species in each community type have an indicator status of OBL, FACW, and/or FAC, the vegetation is hydrophytic. Complete the vegetation section of the data form. Portions of the project area failing this test are usually not wetlands, although under certain circumstances they may have hydrophytic vegetation (follow the problem area wetland determination procedures on p. 55). If hydrophytic vegetation is present, proceed to Step 7.

Step 7. *Determine whether soils must be characterized.* Examine vegetative data collected for each plant community (in Steps 5 and 6) and identify any plant community where: (1) all dominant species have an indicator status of OBL, or (2) all dominant species have an indicator status of OBL and FACW and the wetland boundary is abrupt. For these communities, hydric soils are assumed to be present and do not need to be examined; proceed to Step 9. Plant communities lacking the above characteristics must have soils examined; proceed to Step 8.

Step 8. *Determine whether the hydric soil criterion is met.* Locate the observation area on a county soil survey map, if possible, and determine the soil map unit delineation for the area. Using a soil auger, probe, or spade, make a hole at least 18 inches deep at the representative location in each plant community type. Examine soil characteristics and compare if possible to soil descriptions in the county soil survey report. If soil colors match those described for hydric soil, then record data and proceed to Step 9. If not, then check for hydric

soil indicators below the A-horizon (surface layer) and within 18 inches for organic soils and for mineral soils with low permeability rates (<6.0 inches/hour), within 12 inches for coarse-textured (sandy) mineral soils with high permeability rates ($\geq$6.0 inches/hour), and within 6 inches for somewhat poorly drained soils. (*Note*: If the A-horizon extends below the designated depth, look immediately below the A-horizon for signs of hydric soil.) Are hydric soil indicators present (see pp. 13-15)? If so, list indicators present on an appropriate data form and proceed to Step 9. If soil has been plowed or otherwise altered, which may have eliminated these indicators, proceed to the section on disturbed areas (p. 50). If field indicators are not present, but available information verifies that the hydric soil criterion is met, then the soil is hydric. Complete the soils section on the appropriate data sheet. (*CAUTION*: Become familiar with problematic hydric soils that do not possess good hydric field indicators, such as red parent material soils, some sandy soils, and some floodplain soils, so that these hydric soils are not misidentified as nonhydric soils; see the problem area wetlands discussion on p. 55.)

Step 9. *Determine whether the wetland hydrology criterion is met.* Examine the area of each plant community type for indicators of wetland hydrology (see pp. 17-19). The wetland hydrology criterion is met when:

1) one or more field indicators are present; or

2) available hydrologic records provide sufficient evidence; or

3) the plant community is dominated by OBL, FACW and/or FAC species or has a prevalence index of less than 3.0, and the area has not been hydrologically disturbed.

If the area is hydrologically disturbed, proceed to the section on disturbed areas (p. 50). Record observations and other evidence on the appropriate data form. Proceed to Step 10.

Step 10. *Make the wetland determination.* Examine data forms for each plant community identified in the project area. Each community meeting the hydrophytic vegetation, hydric soil, and wetland hydrology criteria is considered wetland. If all communities meet these three criteria, then the entire project area is a wetland. If only a portion of the project area is wetland, then the wetland-nonwetland boundary must be established. Proceed to Step 11.

Step 11. *Determine the wetland-nonwetland boundary.* Where a base map or annotated photo was prepared, mark each plant community type on the map or photo with a "W" if wetland or an "N" if nonwetland. Combine all "W" types into a single mapping unit, if possible, and all "N" types into another mapping unit. On the map or photo, the wetland boundary will be represented by the interface of these mapping units. If flagging the boundary on the ground, the boundary is established by determining the location where hydrophytic vegetation and hydric soils give way to nonhydrophytic vegetation and nonhydric soils. This will often require sampling a few more holes to better define the limits of the hydric soils and thereby establish the limits of hydrophytic vegetation.

Intermediate-level Onsite Determination Method

4.12. On occasion, a more rigorous sampling method is required than the routine method to determine whether hydrophytic vegetation is present at a given site, especially where the boundary between wetland and nonwetland is gradual or indistinct. This circumstance requires more intensive sampling of vegetation and soils than presented in the routine determination method. This method also may be used for areas greater than five acres in size or other areas that are highly diverse in vegetation.

4.13. The intermediate-level onsite determination method has been developed to provide for more intensive vegetation sampling than the routine method. Two optional approaches are presented: (1) quadrat transect sampling procedure, and (2) vegetation unit sampling procedure. The former procedure involves establishing transects within the project area and sampling plant communities along the transect within sample quadrats, with soils and hydrology also assessed as needed in each sample plot. In contrast, the vegetation unit sampling procedure offers a different approach for analyzing the vegetation. First, vegetation units are designated in the project area and then a meander survey is conducted in each unit where visual estimates of percent areal coverage by plant species are made. Soil

and hydrology observations also are made as necessary. Boundaries between wetland and nonwetland are established by examining the transitional gradient between them.

4.14. The following steps should be completed:

Step 1. *Locate the limits of the project area in the field and conduct a general reconnaissance of the area.* Previously the project boundary should have been determined on aerial photos or maps. Now appropriate ground reference points need to be located to insure that sampling will be conducted in the proper area. In examining the project area, were any significantly disturbed areas observed? If YES, identify their limits for they should be evaluated separately for wetland determination purposes (usually after evaluating undisturbed areas). Refer to the section on disturbed areas (p. 50) to evaluate the altered characteristic(s) (i.e., vegetation, soils, or hydrology); then return to this method to continue evaluating the characteristics not altered. Keep in mind that if at any time during this determination, one or more of these three characteristics is found to have been significantly altered, the disturbed areas procedures should be followed. If the area is not significantly disturbed, proceed with Step 2.

Step 2. *Decide how to analyze plant communities within the project area: (1) by selecting representative plant communities (vegetation units), or (2) by sampling along a transect.* Discrete vegetation units may be identified on aerial photographs, topographic and other maps, and/or by field inspection. These units will be evaluated for hydrophytic vegetation and also for hydric soils and wetland hydrology, as necessary. *If the vegetation unit approach is selected, proceed to Step 3.* An alternative approach is to establish transects for identifying plant communities, sampling vegetation and evaluating other criteria, as appropriate. *If the transect approach is chosen, proceed to Step 4.*

Step 3. *Identifying vegetation units for sampling.* Vegetation units are identified by examining aerial photographs, topographic maps, NWI maps, or other materials or, by direct field inspection. All of the different vegetation units present in the project area should be identified. The subject area should be traversed and different vegetation units specifically located prior to conducting the sampling.

Field inspection may refine previously identified vegetation units, as appropriate. It may be advisable to divide large vegetation units into subunits for independent analysis. (*CAUTION*: In highly variable terrain, such as ridge and swale complexes, be sure to stratify properly.) Decide which plant community to sample first and proceed to Step 7.

Step 4. *Establish a baseline for locating sampling transects.* Select as a baseline one project boundary or a conspicuous feature, such as road, in the project area. The baseline should be more or less parallel to the major watercourse through the area, if present, or perpendicular to the hydrologic gradient (see Figure 4). Determine the approximate baseline length. Proceed to Step 5.

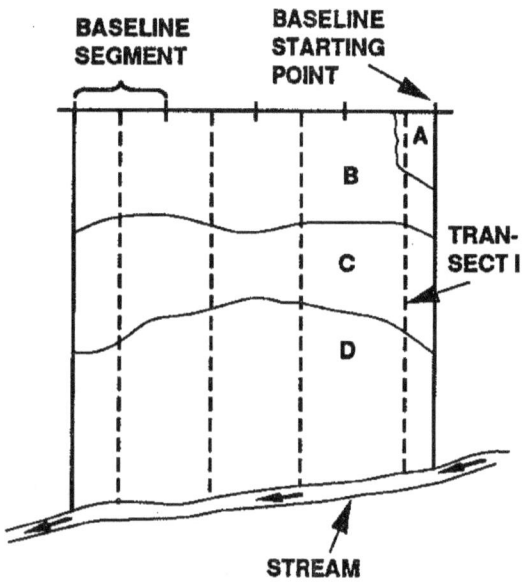

Figure 4. General orientation of baseline and transects (dashed lines) in a hypothetical project area. The letters "A", "B", "C" and "D" represent different plant communities. All transects start at the midpoint of a baseline segment except the first, which was repositioned to include community type A.

Step 5. *Determine the required number and position of transects.* Use the following to determine the required number and position of transects (specific site conditions may necessitate changes in intervals):

Divide the baseline length by the number of required transects to establish baseline segments for sampling. Establish one transect in each result-

Baseline length	Number of Transects
Less than one mile	3
One mile to two miles	3-5
Two miles to four miles	5-8
Four miles or longer	8 or more*

*Transect intervals should not exceed 0.5 mile.

ing baseline segment (see Figure 4). Use the midpoint of each baseline segment as a transect starting point. For example, if the baseline is 1,200 feet in length, three transects would be established: one at 200 feet, one at 600 feet, and one at 1,000 feet from the baseline starting point. *Make sure that all plant community types are included within the transects; this may necessitate relocation of one or more transect lines or establishing more transects.* Each transect should extend perpendicular to the baseline (see Figure 4). Once positions of transect lines are established, go to the beginning of the first transect and proceed to Step 6.

Step 6. *Locate sample plots along the transect.* Along each transect, sample plots are established within each plant community encountered to assess vegetation, soils, and hydrology. When identifying these sample plots, two approaches may be followed: (1) walk the entire length of the transect, taking note of the number, type, and location of plant communities present (flag the location, if necessary), and on the way back to the baseline, identify plots and perform sampling, or (2) identify plant communities as the transect is walked and sample the plot at that time ("sample as you go"). The sample plot should be located so it is representative of the plant community type. When the plant community type is large and covers a significant distance along the transect, select an area that is no closer than 300 feet to a perceptible change in plant community type; mark the center of this area on the base map or photo and flag the location in the field, if necessary. (*CAUTION*: In highly variable terrain, such as ridge and swale complexes, be sure to stratify properly to ensure best results.) At each plant community, proceed to Step 7.

Step 7. *Determine whether normal environmental conditions are present.* Determine whether normal environmental conditions are present by considering the following:

1) Is the area presently lacking hydrophytic vegetation or hydrologic indicators due to annual, seasonal, or long-term fluctuations in precipitation, surface water, or ground-water levels?

2) Are hydrophytic vegetation indicators lacking due to seasonal fluctuations in temperature (e.g., seasonality of plant growth)?

If the answer to either of these questions is *YES* or uncertain, proceed to the section on problem area wetland determinations (p. 55), then return to this method and continue the wetland determination. If the answer to both questions is *NO*, normal conditions are assumed to be present, so proceed to Step 8.

Step 8. *Characterize the vegetation of the vegetation unit or the plant community along the transect.*

If analyzing vegetation units, meander through the unit making visual estimates of the percent area covered for each species in the herb, shrub, sapling, woody vine, and tree strata; alternatively, for the tree stratum determine basal area using the Bitterlich method (Dilworth and Bell 1978; Avery and Burkhart 1983). Then:

1) Within each stratum determine and record the cover class of each species and its corresponding midpoint. The cover classes (and midpoints) are: T = <1% (none); 1 = 1-5% (3.0); 2 = 6-15% (10.5); 3 = 16-25% (20.5); 4 = 26-50% (38.0); 5 = 51-75% (63.0); 6 = 76-95% (85.5); 7 = 96-100% (98.0).

2) Rank the species within each stratum according to their midpoints. (*Note*: If two or more species have the same midpoints and the same or essentially the same recorded percent areal cover, rank them equal; use absolute areal cover values as a tie-breaker only if they are obviously different.)

3) Sum the midpoint values of all species within each stratum.

4) Multiply the total midpoint values for each stratum by 50 percent. (*Note*: This number represents the dominance threshold number and is used to determine dominant species.)

5) Compile the cumulative total of the ranked species in each stratum until 50 percent of the sum of the midpoints (i.e., the dominance threshold number), for the herb, woody vine, shrub, sapling, and tree strata (or alternatively basal area for trees) is immediately exceeded. All species contributing areal cover or basal area to the 50 percent threshold are considered dominants, plus any additional species representing 20 percent or more of the total cover class midpoint values for each stratum or the basal area for tree stratum. (*Note*: If the threshold is reached by two or more equally ranked species, consider them all dominants, along with any higher ranked species. If all species are equally ranked, consider them all dominants.)

6) Record all dominant species on an appropriate data sheet and list indicator status of each. Proceed to Step 9.

If using the transect approach, sample vegetation in each stratum (e.g., tree, shrub, herb, etc.) occurring in the sample plots using the following quadrat sizes: (1) a 5-foot radius for bryophytes and herbs, and (2) a 30-foot radius for trees, saplings, shrubs, and woody vines. Plot size and shape may be changed as necessary to meet site conditions. Determine dominant species for each stratum by estimating one or more of the following as appropriate: (1) relative basal area (trees); (2) areal cover (trees, saplings, shrubs, herbs, woody vines, and bryophytes); or (3) stem density (shrubs, saplings, herbs, and woody vines). (*Note*: Dominant species within each stratum are the most abundant plant species that when ranked in descending order of abundance and cumulatively totaled immediately exceed 50 percent of the total dominance measure for the stratum, plus any additional species comprising 20 percent or more of the total dominance measure.) Record all dominant species on an appropriate data sheet and list the indicator status of each. Proceed to Step 9.

Step 9. *Determine whether the hydrophytic vegetation criterion is met.* When more than 50 percent of the dominant species in the vegetation unit or sample plot have an indicator status of OBL, FACW, and/or FAC, hydrophytic vegetation is present. If the vegetation fails to be dominated by these types of species, the unit or plot is usually not wetland. However, this vegetation unit or plot may constitute hydrophytic vegetation under certain circumstances (refer to the disturbed areas or problem area wetland determination sections on pp. 50-59). If hydrophytic vegetation is present, proceed to Step 10 after completing the vegetation section of the data sheet.

Step 10. *Determine whether soils must be characterized.* Examine vegetative data collected for the vegetation unit or plot (in Steps 8 and 9) and identify any units or plots where: (1) all dominant species have an indicator status of OBL, or (2) all dominant species have an indicator status of OBL and FACW, and the wetland boundary is abrupt. For these units or plots, hydric soils are assumed to be present and do not need to be examined; proceed to Step 12. Vegetation units or plots lacking the above characteristics must have soils examined; proceed to Step 11.

Step 11. *Determine whether the hydric soil criterion is met.* Locate the sample plot or vegetation unit on a county soil survey map if possible, and determine the soil map unit delineation for the area. Using a soil auger, probe, or spade, make a hole at least 18 inches deep in the area. (*Note*: In applying the vegetation unit approach, one or more soil samples should be taken.) Examine soil characteristics in the sample plot or vegetative unit and if possible compare them to soil descriptions in the county soil survey report. If soil colors match those described for hydric soil in the report, then record data and proceed to Step 12. If not, then check for hydric soil indicators below the A-horizon (surface layer) and within 18 inches for organic soils and poorly and very poorly drained mineral soils with low permeability rates (<6.0 inches/hour), within 12 inches for poorly and very poorly drained, coarse-textured (sandy) mineral soils with high permeability rates ($\geq$6.0 inches/hour), and within 6 inches for somewhat poorly drained soils. (*Note*: If the A-horizon extends below the designated depth, look immediately below the A-horizon for signs of hydric soil.) Are hydric soil indicators present (see pp. 13-15)? If so, list indicators present on data form and proceed to Step 12. If soil has been plowed or otherwise altered which may have eliminated these indicators, proceed to the section on disturbed areas (p. 50), then return to this method to continue the wetland determination. If field indicators are not present, but available information verifies that the hydric soil criterion is met, then the soil is hydric. Complete the soils section on an appropriate data sheet. Proceed to Step 12. (*CAUTION*: Become familiar with problematic hydric soils that do not possess good hydric field indicators, such as red parent material soils, some sandy soils, and some flood-plain soils, so that these hydric soils are not misidentified as nonhydric soils; see the section on problem area wetlands, p.55.)

Step 12. *Determine whether the wetland hydrology criterion is met.* Examine the sample plot or vegetation unit for indicators of wetland hydrology (see pp. 17-19) and review available recorded hydrologic information. The wetland hydrology criteria is met when:

1) one or more field indicators are materially present; or

2) available hydrologic records provide necessary evidence; or

3) the plant community is dominated by OBL, FACW, and/or FAC species, *and* the area's hydrology is not significantly disturbed.

If the area's hydrology is significantly disturbed, proceed to the section on disturbed areas (p. 50). Record observations and other evidence on an appropriate data form. Proceed to Step 13.

Step 13. *Make the wetland determination for the plant community or vegetation unit.* Examine the data forms for the plant community (sample plot) or vegetation unit. When the community or unit meets the hydrophytic vegetation, hydric soil, and wetland hydrology criteria, the area is considered wetland. Complete the summary data sheet; proceed to Step 14 when continuing to sample the transect or other vegetation units, or to Step 15 when determining a boundary between wetland and nonwetland plant communities or units. (*Note*: Before going on, double check all data sheets to ensure that the forms are completed properly.)

Step 14. *Sample other plant communities along the transect or other vegetation units.* Repeat Steps 6 through 13 for all remaining plant communities along the transect if following transect approach, or repeat Steps 7 through 13 at the next vegetation unit. When sampling is completed for this transect, proceed to Step 15, or when sampling is completed for all vegetation units, proceed to Step 16.

Step 15. *Determine the wetland-nonwetland boundary point along the transect.* When the transect contains both wetland and nonwetland plant communities, then a boundary must be established.

Proceed along the transect from the wetland plot toward the nonwetland plot. Look for the occurrence of UPL species, the appearance of nonhydric soil types, subtle changes in hydrologic indicators, and/or slight changes in topography. When such features are noted, establish a new sample plot and repeat Steps 8 through 13. (*Note*: New data sheets must be completed for this new plot.) If this area is a nonwetland, move halfway back along the transect toward the last documented wetland plot and repeat Steps 8 through 13, varying plot size as appropriate. Continue this procedure until the wetland-nonwetland boundary point is found. It is not necessary to complete new data sheets for all intermediate points, but data sheets should be completed for each plot immediately adjacent to the wetland-nonwetland boundary point (i.e., data sheets for each side of the boundary). Mark the position of the wetland boundary point on the base map or photo and stake or flag the boundary in the field, as necessary. Continue along the transect until the boundary points between all wetland and nonwetland plots have been established. (*CAUTION*: In areas with a high interspersion of wetland and nonwetland plant communities, several boundary determinations will be required.) When all wetland determinations along this transect have been completed, proceed to Step 17.

Step 16. *Determine the wetland-nonwetland boundary between adjacent vegetation units.* Review all completed copies of the data sheets for each vegetation unit. Identify each unit as either wetland (W) or nonwetland (N). When adjacent vegetation units contain both wetland and nonwetland communities, a boundary must be established. Walk the interface between the two units from the wetland unit toward the nonwetland unit and look for changes in vegetation, soils, hydrologic indicators, and/or elevation. As a general rule, at 100-foot intervals or whenever changes in the vegetation unit's characteristics are noted, establish a new observation area and repeat Steps 8 through 13. (*Note*: New data sheets must be completed for this new area.) If this area is nonwetland, move back down the gradient about halfway back toward the wetland unit and make additional observations along the interface until wetland is identified. (*Note*: Soils often are more useful than vegetation in establishing the wetland-nonwetland boundary, particularly if there is no obvious vegetation break or when FAC plant species dominate two adjacent vegetation units.) At each designated boundary point, complete data sheets for areas immediately upslope and downslope of the wetland-nonwetland boundary (i.e., one set for the wetland unit and one for the nonwetland unit), record the distance and compass directions between the boundary points and their respective pair of soil samples. Mark the position of the wetland boundary point on the base map or photo and stake or flag the boundary in the field, as necessary. Based on observations along the interface, identify a host of boundary points between each wetland unit and nonwetland unit. Repeat this step for all adjacent vegetation units of wetland and nonwetland. When wetland boundary points between all adjacent wetland and nonwetland units have been established, proceed to Step 18.

Step 17. *Sample other transects and make wetland determinations along each.* Repeat Steps 5 through 15 for each remaining transect. When wetland boundary points for all transects have been established, proceed to Step 18.

Step 18. *Determine the wetland-nonwetland boundary for the entire project area.* Examine all completed copies of the data sheets, and mark the location of each plant community type along the transect on the base map or photo, when used. (*Note*: This has already been done for the vegetation unit approach.) Identify each plant community as either wetland (W) or nonwetland (N), if it has not been done previously. If all plant communities are wetlands, then the entire project area is wetland. If all communities are nonwetlands, then the entire project area is nonwetland. If both wetlands and nonwetlands are present, identify the boundary points on the base map and connect these points on the map by generally following contour lines to separate wetlands from nonwetlands. Confirm this boundary by walking the contour lines between the transects or vegetation units, as appropriate. Should anomalies be encountered, it will be necessary to establish short transects in these areas to refine the boundary; make any necessary adjustments to the boundary on the base map and/or on the ground. It also may be worthwhile to flag these boundary points, especially when marking the boundary for subsequent surveying by engineers.

Comprehensive Onsite Determination Method

4.15. The comprehensive determination method is the most detailed, complex, and labor-intensive approach of the three recommended types of onsite determinations. It is usually reserved for highly complicated and/or large project areas, and/or when the determination requires rigorous documentation. Due to the latter situation, this type of onsite determination may be used for areas of any size.

4.16. In applying this method, a team of experts, including a wetland ecologist and a qualified soil scientist, is often needed, especially when rigorous documentation of plants and soils are required. It is, possible, however, for a highly trained wetland boundary specialist to singly apply this method.

4.17. Two alternative approaches of the comprehensive onsite determination method are presented: (1) quadrat sampling procedure and (2) point intercept sampling procedure. The former approach establishes quadrats or sampling areas in the project site along transects, while the latter approach involves a frequency analysis of vegetation at sampling points along transects. The point intercept sampling procedure requires that the limits of hydric soils be established prior to evaluating the vegetation. In many cases, soil maps are available to meet this requirement, but in other cases a qualified soil scientist may need to inventory the soils before applying this method. The quadrat sampling procedure, which involves identifying plant communities along transects and analyzing vegetation, soils, and hydrology within sample plots (quadrats), may be the preferred approach when soil maps are unavailable or the individual is more familiar with plant identification.

Quadrat Sampling Procedure

4.18. Prior to implementing this determination procedure, read the sections of this manual that discuss disturbed area and problem area wetland determination procedures (pp. 50-59); this information is often relevant to project areas requiring a comprehensive determination.

Step 1. *Locate the limits of the project area in the field.* Previously, the project boundary should have been determined on aerial photos or maps. Now appropriate ground reference points need to be located to ensure that sampling will be conducted in the proper area. Proceed to Step 2.

Step 2. *Stratify the project area into different plant community types.* Delineate the locations of these types on aerial photos or base maps and label each community with an appropriate name. (*CAUTION*: In highly variable terrain, such as ridge and swale complexes, be sure to stratify properly to ensure best results.) In evaluating the subject area, were any significantly disturbed areas observed? If *YES*, identify their limits for they should be evaluated separately for wetland determination purposes (usually after evaluating undisturbed areas). Refer to the section on disturbed areas (p. 50) to evaluate the altered characteristic(s) (i.e., vegetation, soils, and/or hydrology); then return to this method to continue evaluating the characteristics not altered. Keep in mind that if at any time during this determination, it is found that one or more or these three characteristics have been significantly altered, the disturbed areas wetland determination procedures should be followed. If the area is not significantly disturbed, proceed to Step 3.

Step 3. *Establish a baseline for locating sampling transects.* Select as a baseline one project boundary or a conspicuous feature, such as a road, in the project area. The baseline ideally should be more or less parallel to the major watercourse through the area, if present, or perpendicular to the hydrologic gradient (see Figure 5). Determine the approximate baseline length and record its origin, length, and compass heading in a field notebook. When a limited number of transects are planned, a baseline may not be necessary provided there are sufficient fixed points (e.g., buildings, walls, and fences) to serve as starting points for the transects. Proceed to Step 4.

Step 4. *Determine the required number and position of transects.* The number of transects necessary to adequately characterize the site will vary due to the area's size and complexity of habitats. In general, it is best to divide the baseline into a number of equal segments and randomly select a point within each segment to begin a transect (see Figure 5).

Use the following as a guide to determine the appropriate number of baseline segments:

Baseline Length (ft)	Number of Segments	Baseline Segment (ft)
<1,000	3	18 – 333
≥1,000 – 5,000	5	200 – 1,000
≥5,000 – 10,000	7	700 – 1,400
>10,000*	variable	2,000

*If the baseline exceeds five miles, baseline segments should be 0.5 mile in length.

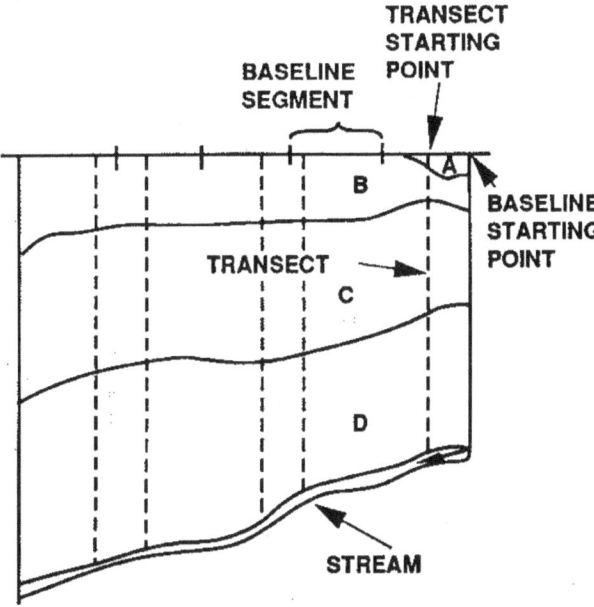

Figure 5. General orientation of baseline and transects in a hypothetical project area. The letters "A", "B", "C", and "D" represent different plant communities. Transect positions were determined using a random numbers table.

Use a random numbers table or a calculator with a random numbers generation feature to determine the position of a transect starting point within each baseline segment. For example, when the baseline is 4,000 feet, the number of baseline segments will be five, and each baseline segment length will be 800 feet (4,000/5). Locate the first transect within the first 800 feet of the baseline. If the random numbers table yields 264 as the distance from the baseline starting point, measure 264 feet from the baseline starting point and establish the starting point of the first transect. If the second random number selected is 530, the starting point of the

second transect will be located at a distance of 1,330 feet (800 + 530) from the baseline starting point. Record the location of each transect in a field notebook. When a fixed point such as a stone wall is used as a starting point, be sure to record its position also. *Make sure that each plant community type is included in at least one transect; if not, modify the sampling design accordingly.* When the starting points for all required transects have been located, go to the beginning of the first transect and proceed to Step 5.

Step 5. *Identify sample plots along the transect.* Along each transect, sample plots may be established in two ways: (1) within each plant community encountered (*the plant community transect sampling approach*); or (2) at fixed intervals (*the fixed interval transect sampling approach*); these plots will be used to assess vegetation, soils, and hydrology.

When employing the plant community transect sampling approach, two techniques for identifying sample plots may be followed: (1) walk the entire length of the transect, taking note of the number, type, and location of plant communities present (flag the locations, if necessary) and on the way back to the baseline, record the length of the transect, identify sample plots and perform sampling; or (2) identify plant communities as the transect is walked, sample the plot at that time ("sample as you go"), and record the length of the transect.

When conducting the fixed interval transect sampling approach, establish sample plots along each transect using the following as a guide:

Transect Length (feet)	Number of Sample Plots	Interval Between the Center of Sample Plots (feet)
<1,000	<10	100
1,000 – <10,000	10	100 – 1,000 (based on length of transect)
≥10,000	>10	1,000

The first sample plot should be established at a distance of 50 feet from the baseline. When obvious nonwetlands occupy a long segment of the transect from the baseline, begin the first plot in the non-wetland at approximately 300 feet from the point where the nonwetland begins to intergrade into a potential wetland community type. Keep in mind that additional plots will be required to determine the wetland-nonwetland boundary between fixed points. In large areas having a mosaic of plant communities, one transect may contain several wetland boundaries.

If obstacles such as a body of water or impenetrable thicket prevent access through the length of the transect, access from the opposite side of the project area may be necessary to complete the transect; take appropriate compass reading and location data. At each sample plot (i.e., plant community or fixed interval area), proceed to Step 6.

Step 6. *Determine whether normal environmental conditions are present.* Determine whether normal environmental conditions are present by considering the following:

1) Is the area presently lacking hydrophytic vegetation or hydrologic indicators due to annual, seasonal or long-term fluctuations in precipitation, surface water, or ground-water levels?

2) Are hydrophytic vegetation indicators lacking due to seasonal fluctuations in temperature (e.g., seasonality of plant growth)?

If the answer to either of these questions is *YES* or uncertain, proceed to the section on problem area wetland determinations (p. 55). If the answer to both questions is *NO*, normal conditions are assumed to be present. Proceed to Step 7 when following the plant community transect approach. If following the fixed interval approach, go to the appropriate fixed point along the transect and proceed to Step 8.

Step 7. *Locate a sample plot in the plant community type encountered.* Choose a representative location along the transect in this plant community. Select an area that is no closer than 50 feet from the baseline or from any perceptible change in the plant community type. Mark the center of the sample plot on the base map or photo and flag the point in the field. Additional sample plots should be established within the plant community at 300-foot intervals along the transect or sooner if a different plant community is encountered. (*Note*: In large-sized plant communities, a sampling interval

larger than 300 feet may be appropriate, but try to use 300-foot intervals first.) Proceed to Step 8.

Step 8. *Lay out the boundary of the sample plot.* A circular sample plot with a 30-foot radius should be established. (*Note* The size and shape of the plot may be changed to match local conditions.) At the flagged center of the plot, use a compass to divide the circular plot into four equal sampling units at 90°, 180°, 270°, and 360°. Mark the outer points of the plot with flagging. Proceed to Step 9.

Step 9. *Characterize the vegetation and determine dominant species within the sample plot.* Sample the vegetation in each layer or stratum (i.e., tree, sapling, shrub, herb, woody vine, and bryophyte) within the plot using the following procedures for each vegetative stratum and enter data on appropriate data sheet (see Appendix B for examples of data sheet):

1) *Herb stratum*

A) Sample this stratum using corresponding approach:

(1) Plant community transect sampling approach:

(a) Select one of the following designs:

(i) Eight (8) - 8" x 20" sample quadrats (two for each sampling unit within the circular plot); or

(ii) Four (4) - 20" x 20" sample quadrats (one for each sample unit within the plot); or

(iii) Four (4) - 40" x 40" sample quadrats (one for each sample unit).

(*Note*: Alternate shapes of sample quadrats are acceptable provided they are similar in area to those listed above.)

(b) Randomly toss the quadrat frame into the understory of the appropriate sample unit of the plot.

(c) Record percent areal cover of each plant species.

(d) Repeat (b) and (c) as required by the sampling scheme.

(e) Construct a species area curve (see example, Appendix C) for the plot to determine whether the number of quadrats sampled sufficiently represent the vegetation in the stratum; the number of samples necessary corresponds to the point at which the curve levels off horizontally; if necessary, sample additional quadrats within the plot until the curve levels off.

(f) For each plant species sampled, determine the average percent areal cover by summing the percent areal cover for all sample quadrats within the plot and dividing by the total number of quadrats (see example, Appendix C). Proceed to substep B below.

(2) *Fixed interval sampling approach:*

(a) Place one (1) - 40" x 40" sample quadrat centered on the transect point.

(b) Determine percent areal coverage for each species. Proceed to substep B below.

B) Rank plant species by their average percent areal cover, beginning with the most abundant species.

C) Sum the percent cover (fixed interval sampling approach) or average percent cover (plant community transect sampling approach).

D) Determine the dominance threshold number - the number at which 50 percent of the total dominance measure (i.e., total cover) for the stratum is represented by one or more plant species when ranked in descending order of abundance (i.e., from most to least abundant).

E) Sum the cover values for the ranked plant species beginning with the most abundant until the dominance threshold number is immediately exceeded; these species contributing to surpassing the threshold number are considered dominants, *plus* any additional species representing 20 percent or more of the total cover of the stratum; denote dominant species with an asterisk on the appropriate data form.

F) Designate the indicator status of each dominant.

2) *Bryophyte stratum* (mosses, horned liverworts, and true liverworts): Bryophytes may be sampled as a separate stratum in certain wetlands, such as shrub bogs, moss-lichen wetlands, and the wetter wooded swamps, where they are abundant and represent an important component of the plant community. If treated as a separate stratum, follow the same procedures as listed for herb stratum. In many wetlands, however, bryophytes are not abundant and should be included as part of the herb stratum.

3) *Shrub stratum* (woody plants usually between 3 and 20 feet tall, including multi-stemmed, bushy shrubs and small trees below 20 feet):

A) Determine the percent areal cover of shrub species within the entire plot by walking through the plot, listing all shrub species and estimating the percent areal cover of each species.

B) Indicate the appropriate cover class (T and 1 through 7) and its corresponding midpoints (shown in parentheses) for each species: T = <1% cover (None); 1 = 1-5% (3.0); 2 = 6-15% (10.5); 3 = 16-25% (20.5); 4 = 26-50% (38.0); 5 = 51-75% (63.0); 6 = 76-95% (85.5); 7 = 96-100% (98.0).

C) Rank shrub species according to their midpoints, from highest to lowest midpoint;

D) Sum the midpoint values of all shrub species.

E) Determine the dominance threshold number - the number at which 50 percent of the total dominance measure (i.e., cover class midpoints) for the stratum is represented by one or more plant species when ranked in descending order of abundance (i.e., from most to least abundant).

F) Sum the midpoint values for the ranked shrub species, beginning with the most abundant, until the dominance threshold number is immediately exceeded; these species are considered dominants, *plus* any additional species representing 20 percent or more of the total midpoint values of the stratum; identify dominant species (e.g., with an asterisk) on the appropriate data form.

G) Designate the indicator status of each dominant.

4) *Sapling stratum* (young or small trees greater than or equal to 20 feet tall *and* with a diameter at breast height less than 5 inches): Follow the same procedures as listed for the shrub stratum or the tree stratum (i.e., plot sampling technique), whichever is preferred.

5) *Woody vine stratum* (climbing or twining woody plants): Follow the same procedures as listed for the shrub stratum.

6) *Tree stratum* (woody plants greater than or equal to 20 feet tall *and* with a diameter at breast height equal to or greater than 5 inches). Two alternative approaches are offered for characterizing the tree stratum:

A) *Plot sampling technique*

This technique involves establishing a sample unit within the 30-foot radius sample plot and determining the basal area of the trees by individual and by species. Basal area for individual trees can be measured directly by using a basal area tape or indirectly by measuring diameter at breast height (dbh) with a diameter tape and converting diameter to basal area using the formula $A = \pi d^2/4$ (where A = basal area, $\pi = 3.1416$, and d = dbh). This technique may be preferred to the plotless technique if only one person is performing a comprehensive determination.

The plot technique involves the following steps:

(1) Locate and mark, if necessary, a sample unit (plot) with a radius of 30 feet, or change the shape of the plot to match topography. (*Note:* A larger sampling unit may be required when trees are large and widely spaced.)

(2) Identify each tree, within the plot, measure its basal area (using a basal area tape) or measure its dbh (using a diameter tape) and compute its basal area, then record data on the data form.

(3) Calculate the total basal area for each tree species by summing the basal area values of all individual trees of each species.

(4) Rank species according to their total basal area, in descending order from largest basal area to lowest.

(5) Calculate the total basal area value of all trees in the plot by summing the total basal area for all species.

(6) Determine the dominant trees species; dominant species are those species (when ranked in descending order and cumulatively totaled) that immediately exceed 50 percent of the total basal area value for the plot, plus any additional species comprising 20 percent or more of the total basal area of the plot; record the dominant species on the appropriate data form.

(7) Designate the indicator status of each dominant (i.e., OBL, FACW, FAC, FACU, or UPL).

B) *Plotless Sampling Technique*

This technique involves determining basal area by using a basal area factor (BAF) prism (e.g., BAF 10 for the East) or an angle gauge to identify individual trees to measure diameter at breast height (dbh) or basal area. This approach is plotless in that trees within and beyond the 30-foot radius plot are recorded depending on their dbh and distance from the sampling point.

(1) Standing near the center of the 30-foot radius plot, hold the prism or angle gauge directly over the center of the plot at a constant distance from the eye and record all trees by species that are "sighted in," while rotating 360° in one direction. (*Note:* Trees with multiple trunks below 4.5 feet should be counted as two or more trees if all trunks are "sighted in." If trunks split above 4.5 feet, count as one tree if "sighted in." Sighting level should approximate 4.5 feet above the ground. With borderline trees, every other tree of a given species should be tallied.)

(2) Measure the dbh of all "sighted in" trees. (*Note:* This should be done as trees are sighted.)

(3) Compute basal area for each tree. (*Note:* When dbh was measured, apply the formula $A = \pi d^2/4$, where A = basal area, $\pi = 3.1416$, and d = dbh. To expedite this calculation, use a hand calculator into which the following conversion factor is

stored - 0.005454 for diameter data in inches or 0.78535 in feet. Basal area in square feet of an individual tree can be obtained by squaring the tree diameter and multiplying by the stored conversion factor.)

(4) Sum the basal areas for individual trees by species, then rank tree species by their total basal area values.

(5) Determine the dominance threshold number by summing the basal areas of all tree species (total basal area for the "plot") and multiplying by 50 percent.

(6) Sum the basal area values for the ranked tree species, beginning with the largest value, until the dominance threshold number is immediately exceeded; all species contributing to surpassing the threshold number are considered dominants, plus any species representing 20 percent or more of the total basal area for the "plot." (*Note*: If it is felt that a representative sample of the trees has not been obtained from one tally, additional tallies can be obtained by moving perpendicular from the center of the plot to another area.) Denote dominant species with an asterisk on the appropriate data form.

(7) Designate the indicator status of each dominant (i.e., OBL, FACW, FAC, FACU, or UPL).

After determining the dominants for each stratum, proceed to Step 10.

Step 10. *Determine whether the hydrophytic vegetation criterion is met.* When more than 50 percent of the dominant species in the sample plot have an indicator status of OBL, FACW, and/or FAC, hydrophytic vegetation is present. Complete the vegetation section of the summary data sheet. If the vegetation fails to be dominated by these types of species, the plot is usually not a wetland, however, it may constitute hydrophytic vegetation under certain circumstances (see the problem area wetland discussion, p. 55). If hydrophytic vegetation is present, proceed to Step 11.

Step 11. *Determine whether the hydric soil criterion is met.* Locate the sample plot on a county soil survey map, if possible, and determine the soil map unit delineation for the plot. Using a soil auger, probe, or spade, make a soil hole at least 18 inches deep (2-3 feet to best characterize most

soils) in the sample plot. Examine the soil characteristics and compare if possible to soil descriptions in the soil survey report. If soil colors match those described for hydric soil in the report, then record data and proceed to Step 12. If not, then check for hydric soil indicators below the A-horizon (surface layer) and within 18 inches for organic soils and poorly drained and very poorly drained mineral soils with low permeability rates (<6.0 inches/hour), within 12 inches for coarse-textured poorly drained and very poorly drained mineral soils with high permeability rates (≥6.0 inches/hour) and within 6 inches for somewhat poorly drained soils. (*Note*: If the A-horizon extends below the designated depth, look immediately below the A-horizon for signs of hydric soil.) If hydric soil indicators are present (see pp. 13-15), list indicators present on data form and proceed to Step 12. If the soil has been plowed or otherwise altered, which may have eliminated these indicators, proceed to the section on disturbed areas (p. 50). If field indicators are not present, but available information verifies that the hydric soil criterion is met, then the soil is hydric.

Complete the soils section on an appropriate data sheet. (*CAUTION*: Become familiar with problematic hydric soils that do not possess good hydric field indicators, such as red parent material soils, some sandy soils, and some floodplain soils, so that these hydric soils are not misidentified as non-hydric soils; see the section on problem area wetlands, p. 55.)

Step 12. *Determine whether the wetland hydrology criterion is met.* Examine the sample plot for indicators of wetland hydrology (see pp. 17-19) and review available recorded hydrologic information. If one or more indicators of wetland hydrology are materially present in the plot, then the wetland hydrology criterion is met. Available hydrologic data may also verify this criterion. Record observations on the appropriate data form and proceed to Step 13. If no such indicators or evidence exist, then wetland hydrology does not occur at the plot; complete the hydrology section on the data sheet.

Step 13. *Make the wetland determination for the sample plot.* Examine the data forms for the plot. When the plot meets the hydrophytic vegetation, hydric soil, and wetland hydrology criteria, it is considered wetland. Complete the summary data sheet; proceed to Step 14 when continuing to sample transects, or to Step 15 when determining a boundary between wetland and nonwetland sample plots. (*Note*: Double check all data sheets to ensure that they are completed properly before going to another plot.)

Step 14. *Take other samples along the transect.* Repeat Steps 5 through 13, as appropriate. When sampling is completed for this transect proceed to Step 15.

Step 15. *Determine the wetland-nonwetland boundary point along the transect.* When the transect contains both wetland and nonwetland plots, then a boundary must be established. Proceed along the transect from the wetland plot toward the nonwetland plot. Look for the occurrence of upland species, the appearance of nonhydric soil types, subtle changes in hydrologic indicators, and/or slight changes in topography. When such features are noted, establish a new sample plot and repeat Steps 8 through 12. (*Note*: New data sheets must be completed for this new sample plot.) If this area is a nonwetland, move halfway back along the transect toward the last documented wetland plot and repeat Steps 8 through 12, varying plot size as appropriate. (*Note*: Soils generally are more useful than vegetation in establishing the wetland-nonwetland boundary, particularly if there is no evident vegetation break or when FAC species dominate two adjacent areas.) Continue this procedure until the wetland-nonwetland boundary point is found. It is not necessary to complete new data sheets for all intermediate points, but data sheets should be completed for each plot immediately adjacent to the wetland-nonwetland boundary point (i.e., one set for each side of the boundary). Mark the position of the wetland boundary point on the base map or photo and place a surveyor flag or stake at the boundary point in the field, as necessary. Continue along the transect until the boundary points between all wetland and nonwetland plots have been established. (*CAUTION*: In areas with a high interspersion of wetland and nonwetland plant communities, several boundary determinations will be required.) When all wetland determinations along this transect have been completed, proceed to Step 16.

Step 16. *Sample other transects and make wetland determinations along each.* Repeat Steps 5 through 15 for each remaining transect. When wetland boundary points for all transects have been established, proceed to Step 17.

Step 17. *Determine the wetland-nonwetland boundary for the entire project area.* Examine all completed copies of the data sheets and mark the location of each plot on the base map or photo. Identify each plot as either wetland (W) or nonwetland (N) on the map or photo. If all plots are wetlands, then the entire project area is wetland. If all plots are nonwetlands, then the entire project area is nonwetland. If both wetland and nonwetland plots are present, identify the boundary points on the base map or on the ground, and connect these points on the map by generally following contour lines to separate wetlands from nonwetlands. Confirm this boundary on the ground by walking the contour lines between the transects. Should anomalies be encountered, it will be necessary to establish short transects in these areas to refine the boundary, apply Step 15, and make any necessary adjustments to the boundary on the base map and/or on the ground. It may be worthwhile to place surveyor flags or stakes at these boundary points, especially when marking the boundary for subsequent surveying by engineers.

Point Intercept Sampling Procedure

4.19. The point intercept sampling procedure is a frequency analysis of vegetation used in areas that may meet the hydric soil and wetland hydrology criteria (see Part II, p. 5). It involves first identifying areas that may meet the hydric soil and wetland hydrology criteria within the area of concern and then refining the boundaries of areas that meet the hydric soil criterion. Transects are then established for analyzing vegetation and determining the presence of hydrophytic vegetation by calculating a prevalence index. Sample worksheets and a sample problem using this method are presented in Appendices B and D, respectively.

Step 1. *Identify the approximate limits of areas that may meet the hydric soil criterion within the area of concern and sketch limits on an aerial photograph.* To help identify these limits use sources of information such as Agricultural Stabilization and Conservation Service slides, soil surveys, NWI maps, and other maps and photographs. (*Note*: This step is more convenient to perform offsite, but may be done onsite.) Proceed to Step 2.

Step 2. *Scan the areas that may meet the hydric soil criterion and determine if disturbed conditions exist.* Are any significantly disturbed areas present? If *YES*, identify their limits for they should be evaluated separately for wetland determination purposes (usually after evaluating undisturbed areas). Refer to the section on disturbed areas (p. 50), if necessary, to evaluate the altered characteristic(s) (vegetation, soils, or hydrology), then return to this method and continue evaluating characteristics not altered. (*Note*: Prior experience with disturbed sites may allow one to easily evaluate an altered characteristic, such as when vegetation is not present in a farmed wetland due to cultivation.) Keep in mind that if at any time during this determination one or more of these three characteristics is found to have been significantly altered, the disturbed area wetland determination procedures should be followed. If the area is not significantly disturbed, proceed to Step 3.

Step 3. *Scan the areas that may meet the hydric soil criterion and determine if obvious signs of wetland hydrology are present.* The wetland hydrology criterion is met for any area or portion thereof where, it is obvious or known that the area is frequently inundated or saturated to the surface during the growing season. If the above condition exists, the hydric soil criterion is met for the subject area and the area is considered wetland. If necessary, confirm the presence of hydric soil by examining the soil for appropriate field indicators. (*Note*: Hydrophytic vegetation is assumed to be present under these conditions, i.e., undrained hydric soil, so vegetation does not need to be examined. Moreover, hydrophytic vegetation should be obvious in these situations.) Areas lacking obvious indicators of wetland hydrology must be further examined, so proceed to Step 4.

Step 4. *Refine the boundary of areas that meet the hydric soil criterion.* Verify the presence of hydric soil within the appropriate map units by digging a number of holes at least 18 inches deep along the boundary (interface) between hydric soil units and nonhydric soil units. Compare soil samples with descriptions in the soil survey report to see if they are properly mapped, and look for hydric soil characteristics or indicators. In this way, the boundary of areas meeting the hydric soil criterion is further refined by field observations. In map units where only part of the unit is hydric (e.g., complexes, associations, and inclusions),

locate hydric soil areas on the ground by considering landscape position and evaluating soil characteristics for hydric soil properties (indicators). (*Note*: Some hydric soils, especially organic soils, have not been given a series name and are referred to by common names, such as peat, muck, swamp, marsh, wet alluvial land, tidal marsh, sulfaquents, and sulfihemists. These areas are also considered hydric soil map units. Certain hydric soils are mapped with nonhydric soils as an association or complex, while other hydric soils occur as inclusions in nonhydric soil map units. Only the hydric soil portion of these map units should be evaluated for hydrophytic vegetation.) In areas where hydric soils are not easily located by landscape position and soil characteristics (morphology), a qualified soil scientist should be consulted. (*CAUTION*: Become familiar with problematic hydric soils that do not possess good hydric field indicators, such as red parent material soils, some sandy soils, and some floodplains soils, so that these hydric soils are not misidentified as nonhydric soils, see section on problem area wetlands, p. 55.) (*Note*: If the project area does not have a soil map, hydric soil areas must be determined in the field to use the point intercept sampling method. Consider landscape position, such as depressions, drainageways, floodplains and seepage slopes, and look for field indicators of hydric soil, then delineate the hydric soil areas accordingly. If the boundary of the hydric soil area cannot be readily delineated, one should use the quadrat sampling procedure on p. 40.)

After establishing the boundary of the area in question, proceed to Step 5.

Step 5. *Determine whether normal environmental conditions are present.* Determine whether normal environmental conditions are present by considering the following:

1) Is the area presently lacking hydrophytic vegetation or hydrologic indicators due to annual, seasonal, or long-term fluctuations in precipitation, surface water, or ground water levels?

2) Are hydrophytic vegetation indicators lacking due to seasonal fluctuations in temperature (e.g., seasonality of plant growth)?

If the answer to either of these questions is *YES* or uncertain, proceed to the section on problem area wetland determinations (p. 55). If the answer to both questions is *NO*, normal conditions are assumed to be present. Proceed to Step 6.

Step 6. *Determine random starting points and random directions for three 200-foot line transects in each area that meets or may meet the hydric soil criterion.* (*Note*: More than three transects may be required depending on the standard error obtained for the three transects.) There are many ways to determine random starting points and random transect direction. The following procedures are suggested:

1) *Starting point* — Superimpose a grid over an aerial photo or map of the study area. Assign numbers (1, 2, 3 ...N) to each vertical and horizontal line on the grid. Starting points for a transect are selected by using a table for generating random numbers or other suitable method. The first selected digit represents a line on the horizontal axis; the second, the vertical axis. The intersection of the two lines establishes a starting point.

2) *Transect direction* — At a starting point, spin a pencil or similar pointed object in the air and let it fall to the ground. The direction that the pencil is pointing indicates the direction of the transect. Proceed to Step 7.

Step 7. *Lay out the transect in the established direction.* If the transect crosses the hydric soil boundary (into the nonhydric soil area), bend the line back into the hydric soil area by randomly selecting a new direction for the transect following the procedure suggested above. Mark the approximate location of the transect on a base map or aerial photo. Proceed to Step 8.

Step 8. *Record plant data (e.g., species name, indicator group, and number of occurrences) at interval points along the transect.* At the starting point and at each point on 2-foot intervals along the transect, record all plants that would intersect an imaginary vertical line extending through the point. If this line has no plants intersecting it (either above or below the sample point), record nothing.

Identify each plant observed to species (or other taxonomic category if species cannot be identified), enter species name on the Prevalence Index Worksheet, and record all occurrences of each species along the transect. For each species listed, identify its indicator group from the appropriate regional list of plant species that occur in wetlands (i.e., OBL, FACW, FAC, FACU, and UPL; see p. 5). Plant species not recorded on the lists are assumed to be upland species. If no regional indicator status and only one national indicator status is assigned, apply the national indicator status to the species. If no regional indicator status is assigned and more than one national indicator status is assigned, do not use the species to calculate a prevalence index. If the plant species is on the list and no regional or national indicator status is assigned, do not use the species to calculate the prevalence index. *For a transect to be valid for a prevalence calculation, at least 80 percent of the occurrences must be plants that have been identified and placed in an indicator group.* Get help in plant identification if necessary. (*Note*: Unidentified plants or plants without indicator status are recorded but are not used to calculate the prevalence index.) Proceed to Step 9.

Step 9. *Calculate the total frequency of occurrences for each species (or other taxonomic category), for each indicator group of plants, and for all plant species observed, and enter on the Prevalence Index Worksheet.* The frequency of occurrences of a plant species equals the number of times it occurs at the sampling points along the transect. Proceed to Step 10.

Step 10. *Calculate the prevalence index for the transect using the following formula:*

$$PI_i = \frac{F_o + 2F_{fw} + 3F_f + 4F_{fu} + 5F_u}{F_o + F_{fw} + F_f + F_{fu} + F_u}$$

where

PI_i = Prevalence Index for transect i;

F_o = Frequency of occurrence of obligate wetland species;

F_{fw} = Frequency of occurrence of facultative wetland species;

F_f = Frequency of occurrence of facultative species;

F_{fu} = Frequency of occurrence of facultative upland species;

F_u = Frequency of occurrence of upland species.

After calculating and recording the prevalence index for this transect, proceed to Step 11.

Step 11. *Repeat Steps 5 through 10 for two other transects.* After completing the three transects, proceed to Step 12.

Step 12. *Calculate a mean prevalence index for the three transects.* To be considered wetland, a hydric soil area usually must have a mean prevalence index (PI_M) of less than 3.0. A minimum of three transects are required in each delineated area of hydric soil, but enough transects are required so that the standard error for PI_M does not exceed 0.20 percent.

Compute the mean prevalence index for the three transects by using the following formula:

$$PI_M = \frac{PI_T}{N}$$

where

PI_M = mean prevalence index for transects;
PI_T = sum of prevalence index values for all transects;
N = total number of transects.

After computing the mean prevalence index for the three transects, proceed to Step 13.

Step 13. *Calculate the standard deviation (s) for the prevalence index* using the following formula:

$$s = \sqrt{\frac{(PI_1-PI_M)^2 + (PI_2-PI_M)^2 + (PI_3-PI_M)^2}{N-1}}$$

(*Note*: See formulas in Steps 8 and 10 for symbol definitions.)

After performing this calculation, proceed to Step 14.

Step 14. *Calculate the standard error (s$\bar{x}$) of the mean prevalence index using the following formula:*

$$s\bar{x} = \frac{s}{N}$$

where

s = standard deviation for the Prevalence Index
N = total number of transects

(*Note*: The s$\bar{x}$ cannot exceed 0.20. If s$\bar{x}$ exceeds 0.20, one or more additional transects are required. Repeat Steps 6 through 14, as necessary, for each additional transect.) When s$\bar{x}$ for all transects does not exceed 0.20, proceed to Step 15.

Step 15. *Record final mean prevalence index value for each hydric soil map unit and make a wetland determination.* All areas having a mean prevalence index of less than 3.0 meet the hydrophytic vegetation criterion (see p. 5). One should also look for evidence or field indicators of wetland hydrology, especially if there is some question as to whether the wetland hydrology criterion is met. If such evidence or indicators are present or the area's hydrology has not been disturbed, then the area is considered a wetland. If the area has been hydrologically disturbed, one must determine whether the area is effectively drained before making a wetland determination (see disturbed area discussion, p. 50). If the area is effectively drained, it is considered nonwetland; if it is not, the wetland hydrology criterion is met and the area is considered a wetland.

Areas where the prevalence index value is greater than or equal to 3.0 (especially greater than 3.5) are usually not wetlands, but can, on occasion, be wetlands. These exceptions are disturbed or problem area wetlands (see discussion on pp. 50-59) and further evaluation of wetland hydrology must be undertaken. When the prevalence index falls between 3.0 and 3.5 (inclusive) in the absence of significant hydrologic modification, the area is presumed to meet the wetland hydrology criterion and is, therefore, wetland; the plant community is considered hydrophytic vegetation since the plants are growing in an undrained hydric soil. If the prevalence index of the plant community is greater than 3.5, stronger evidence of wetland hydrology is required to make a wetland determination. Walk through the area of concern and look for field indicators of wetland hydrology. If field observations, aerial photographs or other reliable sources provide direct evidence of inundation or soil saturation within 6, 12, or 18 inches depending on soil permeability and drainage class for one week or more during the growing season, or if oxidized channels (rhizospheres) are present around living roots and rhizomes of any plants, or if water-stained leaves caused by inundation are present, then these areas are considered to meet the wetland hydrology criteria and are wetlands. If direct evidence or these field indicators are not present, then one must use best professional judgement to make the wetland determination. In doing so, one should review the problem area wetland discussion (p. 55), consider other hydrologic indicators that may be present (see pp. 17-19), and perhaps even consult with a wetland expert to assist in the determination.

Disturbed Area and Problem Area Wetland Determination Procedures

4.20. In the course of field investigations, one will undoubtedly encounter significantly disturbed or altered areas, or natural areas where making a wetland determination is not easy. Disturbed areas include situations where field indicators of one or more of the three wetland identification criteria are obliterated or not present due to recent change. In contrast, there are other wetlands that, under natural conditions, are simply difficult to identify, such as wetlands dominated by FACU species, wetlands lacking field indicators for one or more of the technical criteria for wetlands, and wetlands occurring on difficult to identify hydric soils. These wetlands are considered problem area wetlands. The following sections discuss these difficult, confounding situations and present procedures for distinguishing wetlands from nonwetlands.

Disturbed Areas

4.21. Disturbed areas have been altered either recently or in the past in some way that makes wetland identification more difficult than it would be in the absence of such changes. Disturbed areas include both wetlands and nonwetlands that have been modified to varying degrees by human activities (e.g., filling, excavation, clearing, damming, and building construction) or by natural events (e.g., avalanches, mudslides, fire, volcanic deposition, and beaver dams). Such activities and events change the character of the area often making it difficult to identify field characteristics of one or more of the wetland identification criteria (i.e., hydrophytic vegetation, hydric soils, and wetland hydrology). Disturbed wetlands include areas subjected to deposition of fill or dredged material,

removal or other alteration of vegetation, conversion to agricultural land and silviculture plantations, and construction of levees, channelization and drainage systems, and/or dams (e.g., reservoirs and beaver dams) that significantly modify an area's hydrology. In cases where recent human activities have caused these changes, it may be necessary to determine the date of the alteration or conversion for legal purposes. (*Note*: If the activity occurred prior to the effective date of regulation or other jurisdiction, it may not be necessary to make a wetland determination for regulatory purposes.) In considering the effects of natural events (e.g., a wetland buried by a mudslide), the relative permanence of the change and whether the area is still functioning as a wetland must be considered.

4.22. In disturbed wetlands, field indicators for one or more of the three technical criteria for wetland identification are usually absent. It may be necessary to determine whether the "missing" indicator(s) (especially wetland hydrology) existed prior to alteration. To do this requires review of aerial photographs, existing maps, and other available information about the site, and may involve evaluating a nearby reference site (similar to the original character of the one altered) for indicator(s) of the "altered" characteristic.

4.23. When a significantly disturbed condition is detected during an onsite determination, the following steps should be taken to determine if the "missing" indicator(s) was present before alteration and whether the criterion in question was originally met. Be sure to record findings on the appropriate data form. After completing the necessary steps below, return to the applicable step of the onsite determination method being used and continue evaluating the site's characteristics.

Step 1. *Determine whether vegetation, soils, and/or hydrology have been significantly altered at the site.* Proceed to Step 2.

Step 2. *Determine whether the "altered" characteristic met the wetland criterion in question prior to site alteration.* Review existing information for the area (e.g., aerial photos, NWI maps, soil surveys, hydrologic data, and previous site inspection reports) contact knowledgeable persons familiar with the area, and conduct an onsite inspection to build supportive evidence. The strongest evidence involves considering all of the above *plus* evaluating a nearby reference site (an area similar to the one altered before modification) for field indicators of the three technical criteria for wetland. If a human activity or natural event altered the vegetation, proceed to Step 3; the soils, proceed to Step 4; the hydrology, proceed to Step 5.

Step 3. *Determine whether hydrophytic vegetation previously occurred:*

1) *Describe the type of alteration.* Examine the area and describe the type of alteration that occurred. Look for evidence of selective harvesting, clearcutting, bulldozing, recent conversion to agriculture, or other activities (e.g., burning, discing, the presence of buildings, dams, levees, roads, and parking lots).

2) *Determine the approximate date when the alteration occurred if necessary.* Check aerial photographs, examine building permits, consult with local individuals, and review other possible sources of information.

3) *Describe the effects on the vegetation.* Generally describe how the recent activities and events have affected the plant communities. Consider the following:

A) Has all or a portion of the area been cleared of vegetation?

B) Has only one layer of the plant community (e.g., trees) been removed?

C) Has selective harvesting resulted in the removal of some species?

D) Has the vegetation been burned, mowed, or heavily grazed?

E) Has the vegetation been covered by fill, dredged material, or structures?

F) Have increased water levels resulted in the death of all or some of the vegetation?

4) *Determine whether the area had hydrophytic vegetation communities.* Develop a list of species that previously occurred at the site from existing information, if possible, and determine presence of hydrophytic vegetation. If site-specific data do not exist, evaluate a neighboring undisturbed area (reference site) with characteristics (i.e., vegetation, soils, hydrology, and topogra-phy) similar to the area in question prior to its alteration. Be sure to record the location and major characteristics (vegetation, soils, hydrology, and topography) of the reference site. Sample the vegetation in this reference area using an appropriate onsite determination method to determine whether hydrophytic vegetation is present. If hydrophytic vegetation is present at the reference site, then hydrophytic vegetation is presumed to have existed in the altered area. If no indicators of hydrophytic vegetation are found at the reference site, then the original vegetation at the project area is not considered hydrophytic vegetation. If soils and/or hydrology also have been disturbed, then continue Steps 4, 5, and 6 below, as necessary. Otherwise, return to the applicable step of the onsite determination method being used.

Step 4. *Determine whether or not hydric soils previously occurred:*

1) *Describe the type of alteration.* Examine the area and describe the type of alteration that occurred. Look for evidence of:

A) *deposition of dredged or fill material or natural sedimentation* - In many cases the presence of fill material will be obvious. If so, it will be necessary to dig a hole to reach the original soil (sometimes several feet deep). Fill material will usually be a different color or texture than the original soil (except when fill material has been obtained from similar areas onsite). Look for decomposing vegetation between soil layers and the presence of buried organic or hydric mineral soil layers. In accreting or recently formed sandbars in riverine situations, the soils may support hydrophytic vegetation but lack hydric soil indicators.

B) *presence of nonwoody debris at the surface* - This can only be applied in areas where the original soils do not contain rocks. Nonwoody debris includes items such as rocks, bricks, and concrete fragments.

C) *subsurface plowing* - Has the area recently been plowed below the A-horizon or to depths of greater than 10 inches?

D) *removal of surface layers* - Has the surface soil layer been removed by scraping or natural landslides? Look for bare soil surfaces with exposed plant roots or scrape scars on the surface.

E) *presence of manmade structures* - Are buildings, dams, levees, roads, or parking lots present?

2) *Determine the approximate date when the alteration occurred, if necessary.* Check aerial photographs, examine building permits, consult with local individuals, and review other possible sources of information.

3) *Describe the effects on soils.* Consider the following:

A) Has the soil been buried? If so, record the depth of fill material and determine whether the original soil was left intact or disturbed. (*Note:* The presence of a typical sequence of soil horizons or layers in the buried soil is an indication that the soil is still intact; check description in the soil survey report.)

B) Has the soil been mixed at a depth below the A-horizon or greater than 10 inches? If so, it will be necessary to examine the soil at a depth immediately below the plow layer or disturbed zone.

C) Has the soil been sufficiently altered to change the soil phase? Describe these changes. If a hydric soil has been drained to some extent, refer to Step 5 below to determine whether soil is effectively drained or is still hydric.

4) *Characterize the soils that previously existed at the disturbed site.* Obtain all possible evidence that may be used to characterize soils that previously occurred on the area. Consider the following potential sources of information:

A) *soil surveys* - In many cases, recent soil surveys are available. If so, determine the soils that were mapped for the area. If all soils are hydric soils, it is presumed that the entire area had hydric soils prior to alteration.

B) *buried soils* - When fill material has been placed over the original soil without physically disturbing the soil, examine and characterize the buried soils. Dig a hole through the fill material until the original soil is encountered. Determine the point at which the original soil material begins. Remove 18 inches of the original soil from the hole and look for indicators of hydric soils immediately

below the A-horizon and within 6-18 inches (depending on soil permeability and drainage class). Be sure to record the color of the soil matrix, presence of an organic layer, presence of mottles or gleying, and/or presence of iron and manganese concretions. (*Note:* When the fill material is a thick layer, it might be necessary to use a backhoe or posthole digger to excavate the soil pit.) If USGS topographic maps indicate distinct variation in the area's topography, this procedure must be applied in each portion of the area that originally had a different surface elevation.

C) *plowed soils* - Determine the depth to which the soil has been disturbed by plowing. Look for hydric soil characteristics immediately below this depth.

D) *removed surface layers* - Dig a hole 18 inches deep and determine whether the entire surface layer (A-horizon) has been removed. If so, examine the soil immediately below the top of the subsurface layer (B-horizon) for hydric soil characteristics. As an alternative, examine an undisturbed soil of the same soil series occurring at the same topographic position in an immediately adjacent undisturbed reference area. Look for hydric soil indicators immediately below the A-horizon and within 18 inches of the surface. Record and use these data to determine the presence of hydric soils in substep 5 below.

5) *Determine whether hydric soils were present at the project area prior to alteration.* Examine the available data and determine whether indicators of hydric soils were formerly present. If no indicators and/or evidence of hydric soils are found, the original soils are considered nonhydric soils. If indicators and/or evidence of hydric soils are found the hydric soil criterion has been met. Continue to Step 5 if hydrology also was altered. Otherwise, record decision and return to the applicable step of the onsite determination method being used.

Step 5. *Determine whether wetland hydrology existed prior to alteration or whether wetland hydrology still exists (i.e., is the area effectively drained?).* To determine whether wetland hydrology still occurs, proceed to Step 6. To determine whether wetland hydrology existed prior to the alteration:

1) *Describe the type of alteration.* Examine the area and describe the type of alteration that occurred. Look for evidence of:

A) *dams* - Has recent construction of a dam or some natural event (e.g., beaver activity or landslide) caused the area to become increasingly wetter or drier? (*Note*: This activity could have occurred at a considerable distance from the site in question, so be aware of and consider the impacts of major dams in the watershed above the project area.)

B) *levees, dikes, and similar structures* - Have levees or dikes been recently constructed that prevent the area from periodic overbank flooding?

C) *ditches* - Have ditches been recently constructed causing the area to drain more rapidly?

D) *channelization* - Have feeder streams recently been channelized sufficiently to alter the frequency and/or duration of inundation?

E) *filling of channels and/or depressions (land-leveling)* - Have natural channels or depressions been recently filled?

F) *diversion of water* - Has an upstream drainage pattern been altered that results in water being diverted from the area?

G) *groundwater withdrawal* - Has prolonged and intensive pumping of groundwater for irrigation or other purposes significantly lowered the water table and/or altered drainage patterns?

2) *Determine the approximate date when the alteration occurred, if necessary.* Check aerial photographs, consult with local individuals, and review other possible sources of information.

3) *Describe the effects of the alteration on the area's hydrology.* Consider the following and generally describe how the observed alteration affected the project area:

A) Is the area more frequently or less frequently inundated than prior to alteration? To what degree and why?

B) Is the duration of inundation and soil saturation different than prior to alteration? How much different and why?

4) *Characterize the hydrology that previously existed at the area.* Obtain and record all possible evidence that may be useful for characterizing the previous hydrology. Consider the following:

A) *stream or tidal gauge data* - If a stream or tidal gauging station is located near the area, it may be possible to calculate elevations representing the upper limit of wetland hydrology based on duration of inundation. Consult SCS district offices, hydrologists from the local CE district offices or other agencies for assistance. If fill material has not been placed on the area, survey this elevation from the nearest USGS benchmark. If fill material has been placed on the area, compare the calculated elevation with elevations shown on a USGS topographic map or any other survey map that predates site alteration.

B) *field hydrologic indicators onsite or in a neighboring reference area* - Certain field indicators of wetland hydrology may still be present. Look for water marks on trees or other structures, drift lines, and debris deposits (see pp. 17-19 for additional hydrology indicators). If adjacent undisturbed areas are in the same topographic position, have the same soils (check soil survey map), and are similarly influenced by the same sources of inundation, look for wetland hydrology indicators in these areas.

C) *aerial photographs* - Examine aerial photographs and determine whether the area has been inundated or saturated during the growing season. Consider the time of the year that the aerial photographs were taken and use only photographs taken prior to site alteration.

D) *historical records* - Examine historical records for evidence that the area has been periodically inundated. Obtain copies of any such information.

E) *National Flood Insurance Agency flood maps* - Determine the previous frequency of inundation of the area from national floods maps (if available).

F) *local government officials or other knowledgeable individuals* - Contact individuals who might have knowledge that the area was periodically inundated or saturated.

If sufficient data on hydrology that existed prior to site alteration are not available to determine whether wetland hydrology was previously present, then use the other wetland identification criteria (i.e., hydrophytic vegetation and hydric soils) to make a wetland determination.

5) *Determine whether wetland hydrology previously occurred.* Examine available data. If no indicators of wetland hydrology are found, and other evidence of wetland hydrology is lacking, the original hydrology of the area is not considered wetland hydrology. If wetland hydrology indicators and other evidence of wetland hydrology are found, the area meets the wetland hydrology criterion. Record decision and return to the applicable step of the onsite determination method being used.

Step 6. *Determine whether wetland hydrology still exists.* Many wetlands have a single ditch dissecting them, while others may have an extensive network of ditches. A single ditch through a wetland may not be sufficient to effectively drain it; in other words, the wetland hydrology criterion still may be met under these circumstances. Undoubtedly, when ditches are observed, questions as to the extent of drainage arise, especially if the ditches are part of a more elaborate stream channelization or other drainage project. In these cases and other situations where the hydrology of an area has been significantly altered (e.g., dams, levees, groundwater withdrawals, and water diversions), one must determine whether wetland hydrology still exists. If it is present, the area is not effectively drained. To determine whether wetland hydrology still exists:

1) *Describe the type or nature of the alteration.* Look for evidence of:

A) *dams;*
B) *levees, dikes, and similar structures;*
C) *ditches;*
D) *channelization;*
E) *filling of channels and/or depressions;*
F) *diversion of water; and*
G) *groundwater withdrawal.*

(See Step 5 above for discussion of these factors.)

2) *Determine the approximate date when the alteration occurred, if necessary.* Check aerial photographs, consult with local officials, and review other possible sources of information.

3) *Characterize the hydrology that presently exists at the area.* The following sequence of actions is recommended:

A) *Review existing information* (e.g., stream gauge data, groundwater well data, and recent observations) to learn if data provide evidence that wetland hydrology is still present.

B) *Examine early spring or wet growing season aerial photographs for several recent years and look for signs of inundation and/or soil saturation.* (*Note*: Large-scale aerial photographs, 1:24,000 and larger, are preferred.) These signs of wetness indicate that the area still meets the wetland hydrology criterion. If these signs are observed, return to the applicable step of the onsite determination method being used. If such signs are not present, then one should conduct an onsite inspection as follows.

C) *Inspect the site on the ground, look for field indicators of wetland hydrology, and assess changes in the plant community, if necessary.* If field indicators of wetland hydrology (excluding hydric soil morphological characteristics) are present, then wetland hydrology exists; return to the applicable step of the onsite determination method being used. If such indicators are lacking, then examine the vegetation following an appropriate onsite determination method. If OBL and FACW plant species (especially in the herb stratum) are dominant or scattered throughout the site and UPL species are absent or not dominant, the area is considered to meet the wetland hydrology criterion and remains wetland. If UPL species predominate one or more strata (i.e., they represent more than 50 percent of the dominants in a given stratum) and no OBL species are present, then the area is considered effectively drained and no longer wetland. If the vegetation differs from the above situations, then the vegetation at this site should be compared if possible with a nearby undisturbed reference area, so proceed to substep 3D; if it is not possible to evaluate a reference site and the area is ditched, channelized or tile-drained, go to substep 3E, or else go to substep 3F.

D) *Locate a nearby undisturbed reference site with vegetation, soils, hydrology, and topography similar to the subject area prior to its alteration, examine the vegetation (following an appropriate onsite delineation method), and compare it with the vegetation at the project site. If the vegetation is* similar, (i.e., has the same dominants or the subject area has different dominants with the same indicator status as the reference site) then the area is considered to be wetland -- the wetland hydrology criterion is presumed to be satisfied. If the vegetation has changed to where FACU and UPL species or UPL species alone predominate and OBL species are absent, then the area is considered effectively drained and is nonwetland. If the vegetation is different than indicated above, additional work is required -- go to substep 3E if the area is ditched, channelized, or tile-drained, or to substep 3F if the hydrology is modified in other ways.

E) *Determine the "zone of influence" of the ditch (or drainage structure) and the effect on the water table by using existing SCS soil drainage guides.* Obtain the appropriate guide for the project area's soil(s) and collect necessary field measurements (e.g., ditch or other drainage structure dimensions) to use the guide. The zone of influence is the area affected by the ditch. The size of this zone depends on many factors including ditch dimensions, water budget, and soil type. The guide should help identify the extent of the zone as well as the water table within the zone. If the zone of influence has a water table that fails to meet the wetland hydrology criterion, then the zone is effectively drained and is nonwetland, while hydric soil areas outside of the zone remain wetland. If the wetland hydrology criterion is met within the zone, the entire area remains wetland.

F) *Conduct detailed groundwater studies.* Make direct observations of inundation and soil saturation by establishing groundwater wells throughout the site, being sure to place them in a range of elevations so that the data obtained will be representative of the site as a whole. To maximize field effort, it may be best to collect data during the wetter part of the growing season (e.g., early spring in temperate regions). These direct observations, when made during a normal rainfall year, should show whether the wetland hydrology criterion is met. It is advisable, however, to take measurements over a multi-year period. (*Note:* One must be aware of regional weather patterns. For example, observations made during a number of consecutive dry years may lead to erroneous conclusions about wetland hydrology.)

If wetland hydrology still exists, return to the applicable step in the onsite determination method being used and continue delineating the wetland.

Problem Area Wetlands

4.24. There are certain types of wetlands and/or conditions that may make wetland identification difficult because field indicators of the three wetland identification criteria may be absent, at least at certain times of the year. These wetlands are considered problem area wetlands and not disturbed wetlands, because the difficulty in identification is generally due to normal environmental conditions and not the result of human activities or catastrophic natural events, with the exception of newly created wetlands. Artificial wetlands are also included in this section because their identification presents problems similar to some of the natural problem area wetlands.

4.25. Examples of these problem area wetlands are discussed below. Be sure to learn how to recognize these wetlands.

1) *Wetlands dominated by FACU plant species (or communities with a prevalence index greater than 3.5).* Since wetlands often exist along a natural wetness gradient between permanently flooded substrates and better drained soils, the wetland plant communities sometimes may be dominated by FACU species. Although FACU-dominated plant communities are usually uplands, they sometimes become established in wetlands. In order to determine whether a FACU-dominated plant community constitutes hydrophytic vegetation, the soil and hydrology must be examined. If the area meets the hydric soil and wetland hydrology criteria (see pp. 6-7), then the vegetation is hydrophytic.

In these plant communities, take the following steps to make a wetland determination:

Step 1. *Are 25 percent or more and 50 percent or less of the dominant plants in the plant community OBL, FACW, and/or FAC species, or does the community have a prevalence index greater than 3.5 and less than or equal to 4.0 ?* If the answer is *YES,* then proceed to Step 3. If *NO,* proceed to Step 2.

Step 2. *Is the community located: (1) in a depressional or flat area, (2) along a river, stream or drainageway, or (3) adjacent to a more typical wetland plant community (i.e., where greater than 50 percent of the dominants are OBL, FACW, and/ or FAC, or where the prevalence index is less than or equal to 3.5)?* If *YES,* proceed to Step 3. If *NO,* the plant community is usually nonwetland (proceed to Step 3 if any question). Record the data and return to the applicable step of the onsite determination method being used.

Step 3. *Are hydric soils present?* If *YES*, record the data and proceed to Step 4. If *NO*, then the area is nonwetland and the plant community is not hydrophytic. Record the data and return to the applicable step of the onsite determination method being used. (*CAUTION*: Become familiar with problematic hydric soils that do not possess good hydric field indicators, such as red parent material soils, some sandy soils, and some floodplain soils, so that these hydric soils are not misidentified as nonhydric soils; see pp. 58-59.)

Step 4. Answer the following questions:

1) Is there evidence of inundation or soil saturation during the growing season, as indicated by aerial photographs, recorded hydrologic data, previous site inspections, testimony of reliable persons, or direct observations?

2) Are oxidized channels (rhizospheres) present along the living roots and rhizomes of any plants growing in the area?

3) Are water-stained leaves caused by inundation present in the area?

If the answer is *YES* to one or more of these questions, then the area showing these signs is a wetland. Record the data and return to the applicable step of the onsite determination method being used. If the answer *NO* to all questions, proceed to Step 5.

Step 5. *Use one's best professional judgement in determining whether the FACU-dominated community is wetland or nonwetland. Consider the following questions in making this determination:*

1) Are other indicators of wetland hydrology present? (See pp.17-19.)

2) Are observations being made during the dry time of the year? Would conditions be different enough during the wetter part of growing season to affect the determination?

3) Could this plant community be one of the problem area wetlands listed in the following subsection?

4) Is the dominant vegetation introduced or planted? (*Note*: If *YES*, one may choose to evaluate a nearby reference site having natural vegetation.)

5) Could the plant community reflect succession in a wetland?

6) Are OBL or UPL species present in substantial numbers?

7) If the area is forested, does a nearby reference area (where timber has not been harvested) have a plant community where more than 50 percent of the dominant species from all strata are OBL, FACW, and/or FAC species, or a plant community with a prevalence index of less than 3.0?

8) Is the region experiencing a series of dry years or long-term drought during the natural hydrologic cycle and could vegetation be reflecting this condition? If so, is hydrophytic vegetation present during the wet phase of the cycle?

9) Is the area exposed to wide annual fluctuations in vegetation, i.e., wet season vegetation is hydrophytic, while dry season vegetation is dominated by FACU and UPL species?

10) Is the area designated as wetland on National Wetlands Inventory maps, USGS topographic maps, or other maps?

In making a determination in these situations, it may be advisable to consult a wetland expert. Decide whether the area is wetland or nonwetland, record data, and return to the applicable step of the onsite determination method being used.

2) *Evergreen forested wetlands* - Wetlands dominated by evergreen trees occur in many parts of the country. In some cases, the trees are OBL, FACW, and FAC species, e.g., Atlantic white cedar (*Chamaecyparis thyoides*), black spruce (*Picea mariana*), balsam fir (*Abies balsamea*), slash pine (*Pinus elliottii*), and loblolly pine (*P. taeda*). In other cases, however, the dominant evergreen trees are FACU species, including red spruce

(*Picea rubens*), Engelmann spruce (*P. engelmannii*), white spruce (*P. glauca*), Sitka spruce (*P. sitchensis*), eastern white pine (*Pinus strobus*), pitch pine (*P. rigida*), lodgepole pine (*P. contorta*), longleaf pine (*P. palustris*), ponderosa pine (*P. ponderosa*), red pine (*P. resinosa*), jack pine (*P. banksiana*), eastern hemlock (*Tsuga canadensis*), western hemlock (*T. heterophylla*), Pacific silver fir (*Abies amabilis*), white fir (*A. concolor*), and subalpine fir (*A. lasiocarpa*). In dense stands, these evergreen trees may preclude the establishment of understory vegetation or, in some cases, understory vegetation is also FACU species. Since these plant communities are usually found on nonwetlands, the ones established in wetland areas may be difficult to recognize at first glance. The landscape position of the evergreen forested areas such as depressions, drainageways, bottomlands, flats in sloping terrain, and seepage slopes, should be considered because it often provides good clues to the likelihood of wetland. Soils also should be examined in these situations. For identification, follow procedures for FACU-dominated wetlands described above.

3) *Wetlands on glacial till* - Sloping wetlands occur in glaciated areas where thin soils cover relatively impermeable glacial till or where layers of glacial till have different hydraulic conditions that permit groundwater seepage. Such areas are seldom, if ever, flooded, but downslope groundwater movement keeps the soils saturated for a sufficient portion of the growing season to produce anaerobic and reducing soil conditions. This promotes development of hydric soils and hydrophytic vegetation. Indicators of wetland hydrology may be lacking during the drier portion of the growing season. Hydric soil indicators also may be lacking because certain areas are so rocky that it is difficult to examine soil characteristics within 18 inches.

4) *Highly variable seasonal wetlands* - In many regions (especially in arid and semiarid regions), depressional areas occur that may have indicators of all three wetland criteria during the wetter portion of the growing season, but normally lack indicators of wetland hydrology and/or hydrophytic vegetation during the drier portion of the growing season. In addition, some of these areas lack field indicators of hydric soil. OBL and FACW plant species normally are dominant during the wetter portion of the growing season, while FACU and UPL species (usually annuals) may be dominant during the drier portion of the growing season and

during and for some time after droughts. Examples of highly variable seasonal wetlands are pothole wetlands in the upper Midwest, playa wetlands in the Southwest, and vernal pools along the coast of California. Become familiar with the ecology of these and similar types of wetlands (see Appendix A for readings). Also, be particularly aware of drought conditions that permit invasion of UPL species (even perennials).

5) *Interdunal swale wetlands* - Along the U.S. coastline, seasonally wet swales supporting hydrophytic vegetation are located within sand dune complexes on barrier islands and beaches. Some of these swales are inundated or saturated to the surface for considerable periods during the growing season, while others are wet for only the early part of the season. In some cases, swales may be flooded irregularly by the tides. These wetlands have sandy soils that generally lack field indicators of hydric soil. In addition, indicators of wetland hydrology may be absent during the drier part of the growing season. Consequently, these wetlands may be difficult to identify.

6) *Vegetated river bars and adjacent flats* - Along western streams in arid and semiarid parts of the country, some river bars and flats may be vegetated by FACU species while others may be colonized by wetter species. If these areas are frequently inundated for one or more weeks during the growing season, they are wetlands. The soils often do not reflect the characteristic field indicators of hydric soils, however, and thereby pose delineation problems.

7) *Vegetated flats* - Vegetated flats are characterized by a marked seasonal periodicity in plant growth. They are dominated by annual OBL species, such as wild rice (*Zizania aquatica*), and/or perennial OBL species, such as spatterdock (*Nuphar luteum*), that have nonpersistent vegetative parts (i.e., leaves and stems breakdown rapidly during the winter, providing no evidence of the plant on the wetland surface at the beginning of the next growing season). During winter and early spring, these areas lack vegetative cover and resemble mud flats; therefore, they do not appear to qualify as wetlands. But during the growing season the vegetation becomes increasingly evident, qualifying the area as wetland. In evaluating these areas, which occur both in coastal and interior parts of the country, one must consider the time of year of the field observation and the seasonality of the

vegetation. Again, one must become familiar with the ecology of these wetland types (see Appendix A for readings).

8) *Caprock limestone wetlands* - These wetlands are found in the Everglades region of southern Florida. The substrate, commonly called "rockland," is composed mainly of Miami oolite or Tamiami limestone with a very thin covering of unconsolidated soil material in places. Plant communities are varied ranging from saw grass (*Cladium jamaicense;* OBL) marshes to slash pine (*Pinus elliottii*; FACW) forested wetlands. However, exotic species with drier indicator statuses are invading many areas and replacing native species. These exotics include Brazilian pepper (*Schinus terebinthifolius*; FAC), cajeput (*Melaleuca quinquenervis*; FAC), and Australian pines (*Casuarina* spp.; FACU). These wetlands are inundated annually and the water table is at or near the land surface for prolonged periods, as long as nine months in places. Hydric soils may not be present in many places in these wetlands, since substrate (consolidated material) predominates and little or no soil (unconsolidated material) may exist. Despite the lack of hydric soils in places, these areas are wetlands because they meet the wetland hydrology criterion.

9) *Newly created wetlands* - These wetlands include manmade (artificial) wetlands, beaver-created wetlands, and other natural wetlands. Artificial wetlands may be purposely or accidentally created (e.g., road impoundments, undersized culverts, irrigation, and seepage from earth-dammed impoundments) by human activities. Many of these areas will have indicators of wetland hydrology and hydrophytic vegetation. But the area may lack typical field characteristics of hydric soils, since the soils have just recently been inundated and/or saturated. Since all of these wetlands are newly established, field indicators of one or more of the wetland identification criteria may not be present.

10) *Entisols (floodplain and sandy soils)* - Entisols are usually young or recently formed soils that have little or no evidence of pedogenically developed horizons (U.S.D.A. Soil Survey Staff 1975). These soils are typical of floodplains throughout the U.S., but are also found in glacial outwash plains, along tidal waters, and in other areas. They include sandy soils of riverine islands, bars, and banks and finer-textured soils of floodplain terraces. Wet entisols have an aquic or peraquic moisture

regime and are considered hydric soils, unless effectively drained. Some entisols are easily recognized as hydric soils such as the sulfaquents of tidal salt marshes, whereas others pose problems because they do not possess typical hydric soil field indicators. Wet sandy entisols (with loamy fine sand and coarser textures in horizons within 20 inches of the surface) may lack sufficient organic matter and clay to develop hydric soil colors. When these soils have a hue between 10YR and 10Y and distinct or prominent mottles present, a chroma of 3 or less is permitted to identify the soil as hydric (i.e., an aquic moisture regime). Also, hydrologic data showing that NTCHS criteria #3 or #4 (p. 6) are met are sufficient to verify these soils as hydric. Become familiar with wet entisols and their diagnostic field properties (see "Soil Taxonomy", U.S.D.A. Soil Survey Staff 1975 and county soil surveys).

11) *Red parent material soils* - Hydric mineral soils derived from red parent materials (e.g., weathered clays, Triassic sandstones, and Triassic shales) may lack the low chroma colors characteristic of most hydric mineral soils. In these soils, the hue is redder than 10YR because of parent materials that remain red after citrate-dithionite extraction, so the low chroma requirement for hydric soil is waived (U.S.D.A. Soil Conservation Service 1982). Red soils are most common along the Gulf-Atlantic Coastal Plain (Ultisols), but are also found in the Midwest and parts of the Southwest and West (Alfisols), in the tropics, and in glacial areas where older landscapes of red shales and sandstones have been exposed. Become familiar with these hydric soils and learn how to recognize them in the field (see "Soil Taxonomy", U.S.D.A. Soil Survey Staff 1975 and county soil surveys).

12) *Spodosols (evergreen forest soils)* - These soils, usually associated with coniferous forests, are common in northern temperate and boreal regions of the U.S. and are also prevalent along the Gulf-Atlantic Coastal Plain. Spodosols have a gray eluvial E-horizon overlying a diagnostic spodic horizon of accumulated (sometimes weakly cemented) organic matter and aluminum (U.S.D.A. Soil Survey Staff 1975). A process called podzolization is responsible for creating these two soil layers. Organic acids from the leaf litter on the soil surface are moved downward through the soil with rainfall, cleaning the sand grains in the first horizon then coating the sand grains with organic matter and iron oxides in the second layer. Certain vegeta-

tion produce organic acids that speed podzolization including eastern hemlock (*Tsuga canadensis*), spruces (*Picea* spp.), pine (*Pinus* spp.), larches (*Larix* spp.), and oaks (*Quercus* spp.) (Buol, *et al.* 1980). To the untrained observer, the gray leached layer may be mistaken as a field indicator of hydric soil, but if one looks below the spodic horizon the brighter matrix colors often distinguish nonhydric spodosols from hydric ones. The wet spodosols (formerly called "groundwater podzolic soils") usually have thick dark surface horizons, dull gray E-horizons, and low chroma subsoils. Become familiar with these soils and their diagnostic properties (see "Soil Taxonomy", U.S.D.A. Soil Survey Staff 1975 and county soil surveys).

13) *Mollisols (prairie and steppe soils)* - Mollisols are dark-colored, base-rich soils. They are common in the central part of the conterminous U.S. from eastern Illinois to Montana and south to Texas. Natural vegetation is mainly tall grass prairies and short grass steppes. These soils typically have deep, dark topsoil layers (mollic epipedons) and low chroma matrix colors to considerable depths. They are rich in organic matter due largely to the vegetation (deep roots) and reworking of the soil and organic matter by earthworms, ants, moles, and rodents. The low chroma colors of mollisols are not necessarily due to prolonged saturation, so be particularly careful in making wetland determinations in these soils. Become familiar with the characteristics of mollisols with aquic moisture regimes, since they are usually hydric, unless effectively drained, and be able to recognize these from nonhydric mollisols (see "Soil Taxonomy", U.S.D.A. Soil Survey Staff 1975 and county soil surveys).

4.26. The steps for making wetland determinations in problem area wetlands, except FACU-dominated wetlands, are presented below. (*Note*: Procedures for FACU-dominated communities are on pp. 55-56.) Application of these steps is appro-priate only when a decision has been made during an onsite determination that wetland indicators of one or more criteria were lacking. Specific proce-dures to be used will vary according to the nature of the area, site conditions, and affected criterion. A determination must be based on the best available evidence, including: (1) information obtained from such sources as aerial photos, wetland maps, soil survey maps, and hydrologic records; (2) field data collected during an onsite inspection; and (3) basic knowledge of the ecology of the particular wetland type and associated environmental conditions. (*Note*: The following procedures should only be applied to situations not adequately characterized by the onsite methods in Part IV. Be sure to record necessary information on appropriate data forms.)

Step 1. *Identify each criterion to be reconsi-dered and determine the reason for further consid-eration.* Consider how environmental conditions have affected the criterion in question (hydrophytic vegetation, hydric soil, and/or wetland hydrology). If hydrophytic vegetation is the criterion in ques-tion and the plant community is FACU-dominated, then follow special procedures presented earlier in this section (see pp. 55-56). Proceed to Step 2.

Step 2. *Document available information on each criterion in question.* Examine the available infor-mation and consider personal experience and knowledge of wetland ecology and the range of normal environmental conditions of the area. Con-tact local experts (e.g., government agency and university scientists) for additional information, if possible. Proceed to Step 3.

Step 3. *Determine whether each wetland criteri-on in question is met.* If no information can be found that demonstrates that the wetland criterion in question is satisfied, the area is nonwetland. (*EXCEPTION*: Caprock limestone wetlands do not meet the hydric soil criterion where limestone rock is the predominant substrate; this is an exception to the rule.)

References

Avery, E.T., and H. Burkhart. 1983. FOREST MEASUREMENTS. McGraw-Hill Book Company, Inc., New York, NY.

Bouma, J. 1983. HYDROLOGY AND SOIL GENESIS OF SOILS WITH AQUIC MOISTURE REGIMES. In: L.P. Wilding, N.E. Smeck, and G.F. Hall (editors), PEDOGENESIS AND SOIL TAXONOMY. I. CONCEPTS AND INTERACTIONS. Elsevier Science Publishers, B.V. Amsterdam. pp. 253-281.

Buckman, H.O., and N.C. Brady. 1969. THE NATURE AND PROPERTIES OF SOILS. Macmillian Publishing Company, Ontario, Canada.

Buol, S.W., F.D. Hole, and R.J. McCracken. 1980. SOIL GENESIS AND CLASSIFICATION. The Iowa State University Press, Ames, IO. 406 pp.

Cowardin, L.M., V. Carter, F.C. Golet, and E.T. LaRoe. 1979. CLASSIFICATION OF WETLANDS AND DEEPWATER HABITATS OF THE UNITED STATES. U.S. Fish and Wildlife Service, Washington, DC. Publ. No. FWS/OBS-79/31. 103 pp.

Diers, R., and J.L. Anderson. 1984. PART I. DEVELOPMENT OF SOIL MOTTLING. *Soil Survey Horizons* (Winter): 9-12.

Dilworth, J.R., and J.F. Bell. 1978. VARIABLE PLOT SAMPLING -- VARIABLE PLOT AND THREE-P. Oregon State University Book Stores, Inc., Corvallis, OR.

Environmental Laboratory. 1987. CORPS OF ENGINEERS WETLAND DELINEATION MANUAL. U.S. Army Engineer Waterways Experiment Station, Vicksburg, MS. Tech. Rpt. Y-87-1. 100 pp. plus appendices.

Eyre, F.H. (editor). 1980. FOREST COVER TYPES OF THE UNITED STATES AND CANADA. Society of American Foresters, Washington, DC. 148 pp.

Fowells, H.A. 1965. SILVICS OF FOREST TREES OF THE UNITED STATES. U.S.D.A. Forest Service, Washington, DC. Agricultural Handbook No. 271. 762 pp.

Kollmorgen Corporation. 1975. MUNSELL SOIL COLOR CHARTS. Macbeth Division of Kollmorgen Corp., Baltimore, MD.

Parker, W.B., S. Faulkner, B. Gambrell, and W.H. Patrick, Jr. 1984. SOIL WETNESS AND AERATION IN RELATION TO PLANT ADAPTATION FOR SELECTED HYDRIC SOILS IN THE MISSISSIPPI AND PEARL RIVER DELTAS. In: PROCEEDINGS OF WORKSHOP ON CHARACTERIZATION, CLASSIFICATION, AND UTILIZATION OF WETLAND SOILS (March 26-April 1, 1984). International Rice Research Institute, Los Banos, Laguna, Philippines.

Ponnamperuma, F.N. 1972. THE CHEMISTRY OF SUBMERGED SOILS. *Advances in Agronomy* 24: 29-96.

Reed, P.B., Jr. 1988. NATIONAL LIST OF PLANT SPECIES THAT OCCUR IN WETLANDS: NATIONAL SUMMARY. U.S. Fish and Wildlife Service, Washington, DC. Biol. Rpt. 88(24). 244 pp.

Sipple, W.S. 1987. WETLAND IDENTIFICATION AND DELINEATION MANUAL. VOLUME I. RATIONALE, WETLAND PARAMETERS, AND OVERVIEW OF JURISDICTIONAL APPROACH. U.S. Environmental Protection Agency, Office of Wetlands Protection, Washington, DC. 28 pp. plus appendices.

Sipple, W.S. 1987. WETLAND IDENTIFICATION AND DELINEATION MANUAL. VOLUME II. FIELD METHODOLOGY. U.S. Environmental Protection Agency, Office of Wetlands Protection, Washington, DC. 29 pp. plus appendices.

Tiner, Ralph W., Jr. 1985. WETLANDS OF DELAWARE. U.S. Fish and Wildlife Service, National Wetlands Inventory, Newton Corner, MA. and Delaware Department of Natural Resources and Environmental Control, Wetlands Section, Dover, DE. Cooperative Publication. 77 pp.

Tiner, Ralph W., Jr. 1985. WETLANDS OF NEW JERSEY. U.S. Fish and Wildlife Service, Newton Corner, MA. 117 pp.

Tiner, Ralph W., Jr. 1988. FIELD GUIDE TO NONTIDAL WETLAND IDENTIFICATION. Maryland Department of Natural Resources, Water Resources Administration, Annapolis, MD. and U.S. Fish and Wildlife Service, Region 5, Newton Corner, MA. 283 pp. plus 198 color plates.

Tiner, Ralph W., Jr. and P.L.M. Veneman. 1987. HYDRIC SOILS OF NEW ENGLAND. University of Massachusetts Cooperative Extension, Amherst, MA. Bulletin C-183. 27 pp.

U.S.D.A. Forest Service. 1967. FOREST SURVEY HANDBOOK. National Standards for Forest Inventory. Washington, DC. Forest Service Handbook Series No. 4813.1.

U.S.D.A. Forest Service. 1979. PLANT ASSOCIATIONS OF THE FREMONT NATIONAL FOREST. Pacific Northwest Region, Portland, OR. Publ. No. R6-ECOL-79-004.

U.S.D.A. Forest Service. 1983. FORESTED PLANT ASSOCIATION OF THE OKANAGAN NATIONAL FOREST. Pacific Northwest Region, Portland, OR. Publ. No. R6-ECOL-132b-1983.

U.S.D.A. Forest Service. 1983. PLANT ASSOCIATIONS AND MANAGEMENT GUIDE FOR THE PACIFIC SILVER FIR ZONE. Gifford Pinchot National Forest, Pacific Northwest Region, Portland, OR. Publ. No. R6-ECOL-130a-1983.

U.S.D.A. Forest Service. 1986. PLANT ASSOCIATIONS AND MANAGEMENT GUIDE FOR THE WESTERN HEMLOCK ZONE. Gifford Pinchot National Forest, Pacific Northwest Region, Portland, OR. Publ. No. R6-ECOL-230A-1986.

U.S.D.A. Soil Conservation Service. 1982. HYDRIC SOILS OF THE UNITED STATES. Department of Agriculture. National Bulletin No. 430-2-7. (January 4, 1982).

U.S.D.A. Soil Conservation Service. 1982. NATIONAL LIST OF SCIENTIFIC PLANT NAMES. VOLUME I. LIST OF PLANT NAMES. Washington, DC. SCS-TP-159. 416 pp.

U.S.D.A. Soil Conservation Service. 1982. NATIONAL LIST OF SCIENTIFIC PLANT NAMES. VOLUME 2. SYNONYMY. Washington, DC. SCS-TP-159. 438 pp.

U.S.D.A. Soil Conservation Service. 1987. HYDRIC SOILS OF THE UNITED STATES. 1987. In cooperation with the National Technical Committee for Hydric Soils. USDA-SCS, Washington, DC.

U.S.D.A. Soil Conservation Service. 1988. NATIONAL FOOD SECURITY ACT MANUAL. U.S. Department of Agriculture, Washington, DC.

U.S.D.A. Soil Survey Staff. 1951. SOIL SURVEY MANUAL. U.S. Department of Agriculture, Soil Conservation Service, Washington, DC. Agriculture Handbook No. 18. 502 pp.

U.S.D.A. Soil Survey Staff. 1975. SOIL TAXONOMY. A BASIC SYSTEM OF SOIL CLASSIFICATION FOR MAKING AND INTERPRETING SOIL SURVEYS. U.S. Department of Agriculture, Soil Conservation Service, Washington, DC. 754 pp.

Veneman, P.L.M., M.J. Vepraskas, and J. Bouma. 1976. THE PHYSICAL SIGNIFICANCE OF SOIL MOTTLING IN A WISCONSIN TOPOSEQUENCE. *Geoderma* 15: 103-118.

Glossary

Adaptation - The condition of showing fitness for a particular environment, as applied to characteristics of a structure, function, or entire organism; a modification of a species that makes it more fit for reproduction and/or existence under the conditions of its environment.

Adventitious roots - Roots found on plant stems in positions where roots normally do not occur.

Aerenchymous tissue (Aerenchyma) - A type of plant tissue in which cells are unusually large, resulting in large air spaces in the plant organ; such tissues are often referred to as spongy and usually provide increased buoyancy.

Aerobic - A condition in which molecular oxygen is a part of the environment.

Alfisols - Soils having significantly more clay in the B-horizon than in the A-horizon and high base status.

Anaerobic - A condition in which molecular oxygen is absent (or effectively so) from the environment.

Annual - Occurring yearly or, as in annual plants, living for only one year.

Aqualfs - Soils with an aquic or peraquic moisture regime and having clay accumulating in the B-horizon; wet Alfisols.

Aquents - Soils with an aquic or peraquic moisture regime and lacking distinct soil horizons in the subsoil; wet Entisols.

Aquepts - Soils with an aquic moisture regime and showing some soil development in the B-horizon; wet Inceptisols.

Aquic moisture regime - A moisture condition associated with a seasonal reducing environment that is virtually free of dissolved oxygen because the soil is saturated by ground water or by water of the capillary fringe, as in soils in Aquic suborders and Aquic subgroups.

Aquods - Soils having an accumulation of iron, aluminum, and organic matter in the B-horizon in addition to having an aquic moisture regime; wet Spodosols.

Areal cover - A measure of dominance that defines the degree to which above ground portions of plants cover the ground surface; it is possible for the total areal cover for all strata combined in a community or for single stratum to exceed 100 percent because: 1) most plant communities consist of two or more vegetative strata; 2) areal cover is estimated by vegetative layer; and 3) foliage within a single layer may overlap.

Disturbed condition - As used herein, this term refers to areas in which indicators of one or more characteristics (vegetation, soil, and/or hydrology) have been sufficiently altered by man's activities or natural events so as to make it more difficult to recognize whether or not the wetland identification criteria are met. Artificial wetlands - Wetlands created by the activities of man, either purposefully or accidentally.

Basal area - The cross-sectional area of a tree trunk measured in square inches, square centimeters, etc.; basal area is normally measured at 4.5 feet above ground level and is used as a measure of dominance; the most commonly used tool for measuring basal area is a diameter tape or a D-tape (then convert to basal area).

Baseline - A line, generally a highway, unimproved road, or some other evident feature, from which sampling transects extend into a site for which a jurisdictional wetland determination is to be made.

Bench mark - A fixed, more or less permanent reference point or object of known elevation; the U.S. Geological Survey (USGS) installs brass caps in bridge abutments or otherwise permanently sets bench marks at convenient locations nationwide; the elevations on these marks are referenced to the National Geodetic Vertical Datum (NGVD), also commonly known as mean sea level (MSL); locations of these bench marks on USGS topographic maps are shown as small triangles; since the marks are sometimes destroyed by construction or vandalism, the existence of any bench mark should be field verified before planning work which relies on a particular reference point; the USGS or local state surveyors office can provide information on the existence, exact location and exact elevation of bench marks.

Biennial - An event that occurs at 2-year intervals.

Bog - A shrub peatland dominated by ericaceous shrubs (Family *Ericaceae*), sedges, and peat moss (*Sphagnum* spp.) and usually having a saturated water regime or a forested peatland dominated by evergreen trees (usually spruces and firs) and/or larch (*Larix laricina*).

Boreal region - The geographical area just below the arctic tundra and usually characterized by evergreen forests.

Bryophytes - A major taxonomic group of nonvascular plants comprised of true liverworts, horned liverworts, and mosses.

Buried soil - Soil covered by an alluvial, loessal, or other deposit (including manmade), usually to a depth greater than the thickness of the solum.

Buttressed - The swollen or enlarged bases of trees developed in response to conditions of prolonged inundation.

Capillary fringe - A zone immediately above the water table in which water is drawn upward from the water table by capillary action.

Chemical reduction - Any process by which one compound or ion acts as an electron donor; in such cases, the valence state of the electron donor is decreased.

Chroma - The relative purity or saturation of a color; intensity of distinctive hue as related to grayness; one of the three variables of color.

Comprehensive wetland determination - A type of wetland determination that is based on the strongest possible evidence, requiring the collection of quantitative data for all three wetland identification criteria.

Concretion - A localized concentration of chemical compounds (e.g., calcium carbonate and iron oxide) in the form of a grain or nodule of varying size, shape, hardness, and color; concretions of significance in hydric soils are usually iron oxides and manganese oxides occurring at or near the soil surface, which have developed under conditions of fluctuating water tables.

Contour - An imaginary line of constant elevation on the ground surface; the corresponding line on a map is called a "contour line".

Cover class - A category into which plant species would fit based upon their percent areal cover; the cover classes used (midpoints in parentheses) are T = <1% cover (0), 1 = 1-5% (3.0), 2 = 6-15% (10.5), 3 = 16-25% (20.5), 4 = 26-50% (38.0), 5 = 51-75% (63.0), 6 = 76-95% (85.5), 7 = 96-100% (98.0).

Criteria - Technical requirements upon which a judgment or decision may be based.

Deepwater habitat - Any open water area in which the mean water depth exceeds 6.6 feet at mean low water in nontidal and freshwater tidal areas, or is below extreme low water at spring tides in salt and brackish tidal areas, or the maximum depth of emerging vegetation, whichever is greater.

Density - The number of individuals per unit area.

Detritus - Fragments of plant parts found on the soil surface or in water; when fused together by algae or soil particles, this detritus is an indicator that the soil surface was recently inundated.

Diameter at breast height (dbh) - The width of a plant stem (e.g., tree trunk) as measured at 4.5 feet above the ground surface.

Dike - An embankment (usually of earth) constructed to keep water in or out of a given area.

Disturbed area - An area where vegetation, soil, and/or hydrology have been significantly altered, thereby making a wetland determination difficult.

Dominance - As used herein, refers to the spatial extent of a species; commonly the most abundant species in each vegetation stratum that, when ranked in descending order of abundance and cumulatively totaled, immediately exceeds 50 percent of the total dominance measure (e.g., areal cover or basal area) for the stratum, plus any additional species comprising 20 percent or more of the total dominance measure for the stratum.

Dominance measure - The means or method by which dominance is established, including areal coverage and basal area; the total dominance measure is the sum total of the dominance measure values for all species comprising a given stratum.

Dominance threshold number - The number at which 50 percent of the total dominance measure for a given stratum is represented by one or more plant species when ranked in descending order of abundance (i.e., from most to least abundant); when this number is immediately exceeded, the dominant species for the stratum are realized.

Dominant species - For each stratum, dominant species are those that, when ranked in descending rank order and cumulatively totaled, immediately exceed 50 percent of the total dominance measure (i.e., the dominance threshold number), plus any additional species comprising 20 percent or more of the total dominance measure for the stratum.

Drained, effectively - A condition where ground or surface water has been removed by artificial means to the point that an area no longer meets the wetland hydrology criterion.

Drift line - An accumulation of water-carried debris along a contour or at the base of vegetation that provides direct evidence of prior inundation and often indicates the directional flow of flood waters.

Duff - The matted, partly decomposed, organic surface layer of forested soils.

Duration (of inundation or soil saturation) - The length of time that water stands above the soil surface (inundation), or that water fills most soil pores near the soil surface; as used herein, "duration" refers to a period during the growing season.

Entisols - Soils of slight or recent development; common along rivers and floodplains.

Evergreen (plant) - Retaining its leaves at the end of the growing season and usually remaining green through the winter.

Facultative species - Species that can occur both in wetlands and uplands; there are three subcategories of facultative species: (1) *facultative wetland plants* (FACW) that usually occur in wetlands (estimated probability 67-99%), but occasionally are found in nonwetlands, (2) *facultative plants* (FAC) that are equally likely to occur in wetlands or nonwetlands (estimated probability 34-66%), and (3) *facultative upland plants* (FACU) that usually occur in nonwetlands (estimated probability 67-99%), but occasionally are found in wetlands (estimated probability 1-33%).

Fern allies - A group of nonflowering vascular plants comprised of clubmosses (Family Lycopodiaceae), small clubmosses (Family Selaginellaceae), and quillworts (Family Isoetaceae).

Fibrists - Organic soils (peats) in which plant remains show very little decomposition and retain their original shape; more than two-thirds of the fibers remain after rubbing the materials between the fingers.

Flooded - A condition in which the soil surface is temporarily covered with flowing water from any source, such as streams overflowing their banks, runoff from adjacent or surrounding slopes, inflow from high tides, or any combination of sources.

Flooding, frequent - Flooding is likely to occur often during usual weather conditions (i.e., more that a 50 percent chance of flooding in any year, or more than 50 times in 100 years).

Flora - A list or manual of all plant species that may occur in an area.

Fluvents - Floodplain soils, characterized by buried horizons and irregularly decreasing amounts of organic matter with depth.

Forbs - Broad-leaved herbs, in contrast to bryophytes, ferns, fern allies, and graminoids.

Frequency (of inundation or soil saturation) - The periodicity of coverage of an area by surface water or saturation of the soil; it is usually expressed as the number of years the soil is inundated or saturated during part of the growing season of the prevalent vegetation (e.g., 50 years per 100 years) or as a 1-, 2-, 5-year, etc., inundation frequency.

Frequency analysis - A method of evaluating vegetation in an area by establishing a transect and counting the occurrences of plant species at various sampling points along the transect.

Frequency of occurrence - The number of times a given plant species occurs at sample points along a transect.

Gleization - A process in saturated or nearly saturated soils which involves the reduction of iron, its segregation into mottles and concretions, or its removal by leaching from the gleyed horizon.

Gleyed - A soil condition resulting from gleization which is manifested by the presence of neutral grey, bluish or greenish colors through the soil matrix or in mottles (spots or streaks) among other colors.

Graminoids - Grasses (Family Gramineae or Poaceae) and grasslike plants such as sedges (Family Cyperaceae) and rushes (Family Juncaceae).

Ground water - That portion of the water below the surface of the ground whose pressure is greater than atmospheric pressure.

Growing season - The portion of the year when soil temperatures are above biologic zero (41° F) as defined by "Soil Taxonomy;" the following growing season months are assumed for each of the soil temperature regimes: (1) thermic (February-October); (2) mesic (March-October); (3) frigid (May-September); (4) cryic (June-August); (5) pergelic (July-August); (6) isohyperthermic (January-December); (7) hyperthermic (February-December), (8) isothermic (January-December) and (9) isomesic (January-December).

Hardpan - A very dense soil layer caused by compaction or cementation of soil particles by organic matter, silica, sesquioxides, or calcium carbonate, for example.

Hemists - Organic soils (mucky peats and peaty mucks) in which plant remains show a fair amount of decomposition; between one-third and two-thirds of the fibers are still visible upon rubbing the material between the fingers.

Herb - Nonwoody (herbaceous) plants including graminoids (grass and grasslike plants), forbs, ferns, fern allies, and nonwoody vines; for the purposes of this manual, seedlings of woody plants that are less than three feet in height are also considered herbs.

Herb stratum - Any vegetative layer of a plant community that is composed predominantly of herbs.

Histic epipedon - A 8- to 16-inch soil layer at or near the surface that is saturated for 30 consecutive days or more during the growing season in most years and contains a minimum of 20 percent organic matter when no clay is present or a minimum of 30 percent of organic matter when 60 percent or more clay is present; generally a thin horizon of peat or muck if the soil has not been plowed.

Histosols - An order in "Soil Taxonomy" (Soil Survey Staff 1975) composed of organic soils (mucks and peats) that have organic soil materials in more than half of the upper 32 inches or that are of any thickness if overlying rock.

Horizon - A distinct layer of soil, more or less parallel with the soil surface, having similar properties such as color, texture, and permeability; the soil profile is subdivided into the following major horizons: A-horizon, characterized by an accumulation of organic material; B-horizon, characterized by relative accumulation of clay, iron, organic matter, or aluminum; and the C-horizon, the undisturbed and unaltered parent material. (*Note*: Some soils have an E-horizon, characterized by leaching of organic and other material.)

Hue - A characteristic of color related to one of the main spectral colors (red, yellow, green, blue, or purple), or various combinations of these principle colors; one of the three variables of color; each color chart in the Munsell Soil Color Charts (Kollmorgen Corporation 1975) represents a specific hue.

Hydric soil - A soil that is saturated, flooded, or ponded long enough during the growing season to develop anaerobic conditions in the upper part.

Hydrology - The science dealing with the properties, distribution, and circulation of water.

Hydrophyte - Any macrophyte that grows in water or on a substrate that is at least periodically deficient in oxygen as a result of excessive water content; plants typically found in wetlands and other aquatic habitats.

Hydrophytic vegetation - Plant life growing in water or on a substrate that is at least periodically deficient in oxygen as a result of excessive water content.

Hypertrophied lenticels - An exaggerated (oversized) pore on the stem of woody plants through which gases are exchanged between the plant and the atmosphere; serving to increase oxygen to plant roots during periods of inundation or soil saturation.

Indicator - An event, entity, or condition that typically characterizes a prescribed environment or situation; indicators determine or aid in determining whether or not certain stated circumstances exist or criteria are satisfied.

Inundation - A condition in which water temporarily or permanently covers a land surface.

Levee - A natural or manmade feature of the landscape that restricts movement of water into or through an area.

Litter - The undecomposed plant and animal material found above the duff layer on the forest floor.

Long duration (flooding) - A duration class in which inundation for a single event ranges from 7 days to 1 month.

Macrophyte - Any plant species that can be readily observed without the aid of optical magnification, including all vascular plant species and bryophytes (e.g., *Sphagnum* spp.), as well as large algae (e.g. *Chara* spp., and *Fucus* spp.).

Manmade wetland - Any wetland area that has been purposely or accidentally created by some activity of man; also called artificial wetlands.

Map unit - A portion of a map that depicts an area having some common characteristic.

Matrix - The natural soil material composed of both mineral and organic matter; matrix color refers to the predominant color of the soil in a particular horizon.

Microbial - Pertaining to work by microorganisms too small to be seen with the naked eye.

Mineral soil - Any soil consisting primarily of mineral (sand, silt, and clay) material, rather than organic matter.

Mollisols - Grassland soils of steppes and prairies characterized by deep topsoil (mollic epipedon); common in the Great Plains of the West.

Morphological adaptation - A structural feature that aids in fitting a species to its particular environment (e.g., buttressed bases, adventitious roots, and aerenchymous tissue).

Morphological features - Properties related to the external structure of soil (such as color and texture) or of plants.

Moss-lichen wetland - A wetland dominated by mosses (mainly peat mosses) and lichens with little taller vegetation.

Mottles - Spots or blotches of different color or shades of color interspersed within the dominant matrix color in a soil layer; distinct mottles are readily seen and easily distinguished from the color of the matrix; prominent mottles are obvious and mottling is one of the outstanding features of the horizon.

Nonhydric soil - A soil that has developed under predominantly aerobic soil conditions.

Nonpersistent vegetation - Plants that break down readily after the growing season; no evidence of previous year's growth at beginning of next growing season.

Nontidal - Not influenced by tides.

Nonwetland - Any area that has sufficiently dry conditions that hydrophytic vegetation, hydric soils, and/or wetland hydrology are lacking; it includes upland as well as former wetlands that are effectively drained.

Normal circumstances - Refers to the soil and hydrology conditions that are normally present, without regard to whether the vegetation has been removed.

Obligate wetland species - A plant species that is nearly always found in wetlands; its frequency of occurrence in wetlands is 99% or more.

Offsite determination method - A technique for making a wetland determination in the office.

Onsite determination method - A technique for making a wetland determination in the field.

Organic soil - See Histosols.

Overbank flooding - Any situation in which inundation occurs as a result of the water level of a river or stream rising above bank level.

Oxidation-reduction process - A complex of biochemical reactions in soil that influences the valence state of elements and their ions found in the soil; long periods of soil saturation during the growing season tend to elicit anaerobic conditions that shift the overall process to a reducing condition.

Oxidized rhizospheres - Oxidized channels and soil surrounding living roots and rhizomes of hydrophytic plants.

Parent material - The unconsolidated and more or less weathered mineral or organic matter from which the soil profile is developed.

Pedogenic - Related to soil-building processes occurring within the soil.

Peraquic moisture regime - A soil condition in which reducing conditions always occur due to the presence of ground water at or near the soil surface.

Perennial (plant) - Living for many years.

Periodically - Used herein, to define detectable regular or irregular saturated soil conditions or inundation, resulting from ponding of ground water, precipitation, overland flow, stream flooding, or tidal influences that occur(s) with hours, days, weeks, months, or even years between events.

Permanently flooded - A water regime condition where standing water covers the land surface throughout the year (but may be absent during extreme droughts).

Permeability - The quality of the soil that enables water to move downward through the profile, measured as the number of inches per hour that water moves downward through the saturated soil.

Phase, soil - A subdivision of a series based on features such as slope, surface texture, stoniness, and thickness.

Physiological adaptation - A peculiarity of the basic physical and chemical activities that occur in cells and tissues of a species, which results in it being better fitted to its environment (e.g., ability to absorb nutrients under low oxygen tensions).

Plant community - The plant populations existing in a shared habitat or environment.

Playa - Periodically flooded wetland basin common in parts of the Southwest.

Pneumatophore - Modified roots rising above ground that may function as a respiratory organ in species subjected to frequent inundation or soil saturation.

Podzolization - The process by which sesquioxides (aluminum and iron) are leached from the A-horizon and precipitated in the B-horizon, often resulting in a leached layer, the E-horizon.

Polymorphic (leaves) - Two or more different types of leaves formed on plants; in wetland plants, polymorphic leaves may develop due to extended flooding.

Ponded - A condition in which free water covers the soil surface, for example, in a closed depression; the water is removed only by percolation, evaporation, or transpiration.

Poorly drained - A condition in which water is removed from the soil so slowly that the soil is saturated periodically during the growing season or remains wet for long periods greater than 7 days.

Pothole - A depressional wetland commonly found in Upper Midwest (North and South Dakota and western Minnesota) and similar wetlands found elsewhere.

Prevalence index - A weighted average measure of the sum of the frequency of occurrences of all species along a single transect or as calculated for a plant community by averaging the prevalence index of all sample transects through the community.

Problem area wetland - A wetland that is difficult to identify because it may lack indicators of wetland hydrology and/or hydric soils, or its dominant plant species are more common in nonwetlands.

Profile - Vertical section of the soil through all its horizons and extending into the parent material.

Quadrat - Sample units or plots that vary in size, shape, number, and arrangements, depending on the nature of the vegetation, site conditions, and purpose of study.

Quantitative - A precise measurement or determination expressed numerically.

Range - The set of conditions throughout which an organism (e.g., plant species) naturally occurs.

Reduction - The process of changing an element from a higher to a lower oxidation state as in the reduction of ferric (Fe^{3+}) iron into ferrous iron (Fe^{2+}).

Relative basal area - An estimate of basal area for trees, such as produced by the Bitterlich sampling technique.

Relief - The change in elevation of a land surface between two points; collectively, the configuration of the earth's surface, including such features as hills and valleys.

Reproductive adaptation - A peculiarity of the reproductive mechanism of a species that results in it being better fitted to its environment (e.g., prolonged seed dormancy).

Rhizosphere - The zone of soil in which interactions between living plant roots and microorganisms occur.

Salic horizon - A layer 6 inches or more thick comprised of secondary soluble salts.

Salorthids - Soils of arid regions with a salic horizon within 30 inches of the surface and saturated within 40 inches for one month or more in most years; common in playas of the Southwest.

Sample plot - As used herein, an observation point at which a wetland determination is made.

Sapling - Woody vegetation between 0.4 and 5.0 inches in diameter at breast height and greater than or equal to 20 feet in height, exclusive of woody vines.

Saprists - Organic soils (mucks) in which most of the plant material is decomposed and the original constituents cannot be recognized; less than one-third of the fibers remain visible upon rubbing the material between the fingers.

Saturated - A condition in which all easily drained voids (pores) between soil particles are temporarily or permanently filled with water; significant saturation during the growing season is considered to be usually one week or more.

Seedling - A young tree that is generally less than 3 feet high.

Shrub - Woody vegetation usually greater than 3 feet but less than 20 feet tall, including multi-stemmed, bushy shrubs and small trees and saplings. (*Note*: Woody seedlings less than 3 feet tall are considered part of the herbaceous layer.)

Soil - Unconsolidated material on the earth's surface that supports or is capable of supporting plants out-of-doors.

Soil horizon - A layer of soil or soil material approximately parallel to the land surface and differing from adjacent genetically related layers in physical, chemical, and biological properties or characteristics (e.g., color, structure, and texture).

Soil matrix - The portion of a given soil having the dominant color; in most cases, the matrix will be the portion of the soil having more than 50 percent of the same color.

Soil permeability - The ease with which gases, liquids, or plant roots penetrate or pass through a layer of soil.

Soil phase - A subdivision of a soil series having features (e.g., slope, surface texture, and stoniness) that affect the use and management of the soil, but which do not vary sufficiently to differentiate it as a separate series.

Soil pore - An area within soil occupied by either air or water, resulting from the arrangement of individual soil particles or peds.

Soil profile - A vertical section of the soil through all its horizons and extending into the parent material.

Soil series - A group of soils having horizons similar in differentiating characteristics and arrangements in the soil profile, except for texture of the surface layer.

Soil structure - The combination or arrangement of primary soil particles into secondary particles, units, or peds.

Soil surface - The upper limits of the soil profile; for mineral soils, the upper limits of the highest mineral horizon (A-horizon); for organic soils, the upper limit of undecomposed organic matter.

Soil texture - The relative proportions of the various sizes of particles (silt, sand and clay) in a soil.

Somewhat poorly drained - A condition in which water is removed slowly enough that the soil is wet for significant periods during the growing season.

Species area curve - The curve on a graph produced when plotting the cumulative number of plant species found in a series of quadrats against the cumulative number or area of those quadrats; it is used to determine the number of quadrats sufficient to adequately survey the herb stratum.

Spodic horizon - A subsurface layer of soil characterized by the accumulation of aluminum oxides (with or without iron oxides) and organic matter; a diagnostic horizon for Spodosols.

Stratigraphy - A term referring to the origin, composition, distribution, and succession of geologic strata (layers).

Stratum - A layer of vegetation used to determine dominant species in a plant community.

Suborder (soils) - Second highest taxonomic level of the current U.S. soil classification system.

Substrate - nonsoil.

Surface water - Water present above the substrate or soil surface.

Temperate region - The geographic area having a climate that is neither very hot nor very cold.

Tidal - A situation in which the water level periodically fluctuates due to the action of lunar (moon) and solar (sun) forces upon the rotating earth.

Topography - The configuration of a surface, including its relief and the position of its natural and man-made features.

Transect - A line on the ground along which sample plots or points are established for collecting vegetation data and in many cases, soil and hydrology data as well.

Translocation - The transfer of matter from one location to another within the soil.

Transpiration - The process in plants by which water is released into the gaseous environment (atmosphere), primarily through stomata.

Tree - A woody plant 5 inches or greater in diameter at breast height and 20 feet or taller.

Typical - That which normally, usually, or commonly occurs.

Ultisols - Highly weathered soils having significantly more clay in the B-horizon than in the A-horizon and having low base status; acidic soils common in the Southeast.

Unconsolidated parent material - Material from which a soil develops.

Upland - Any area that does not qualify as a wetland because the associated hydrologic regime is not sufficiently wet to elicit development of vegetation, soils, and/or hydrologic characteristics associated with wetlands. Such areas occurring in floodplains are more appropriately termed nonwetlands.

Value (soil color) - The relative lightness or intensity of color; approximately a function of the square root of the total amount of light; one of the three variables of color.

Vascular (plant) - Possessing a well-developed system of conducting tissue to transport water, mineral salts, and foods within the plant.

Vegetation - The sum total of macrophytes that occupy a given area.

Vegetation unit - A patch, grouping, or zone of plants evident in overall plant cover, which appears distinct from other such units because of the vegetation's structure and floristic composition; a given unit is typically topographically distinct and typically has a rather uniform soil, except possibly for relatively dry microsites (e.g., tree bases, old tree stumps, mosquito ditch spoil piles, and small earth hummocks) in an otherwise wet area or relatively wet microsites (e.g., small depressions) in an otherwise dry area.

Very long duration (flooding) - A duration class in which inundation for a single event is greater than 1 month.

Vertisols - Shrinking and swelling dark clay soils; most common in Texas.

Very poorly drained - A condition in which water is removed from the soil so slowly that free water remains at or on the surface during most of the growing season.

Water mark - A line on vegetation or other upright structures that represents the maximum height reached in an inundation event.

Water table - The zone of saturation at the highest average depth during the wettest season; it is at least six inches thick and persists in the soil for more than a few weeks.

Wetlands - As used herein, areas that under normal circumstances have hydrophytic vegetation, hydric soils, and wetland hydrology.

Wetland boundary - The point on the ground at which a shift from wetlands to nonwetlands occurs.

Wetland determination - The process by which an area is identified as a wetland or nonwetland.

Wetland hydrology - In general terms, permanent or periodic inundation or prolonged soil saturation sufficient to create anaerobic conditions in the soil.

Wetland indicator status - The exclusiveness with which a plant species occurs in wetlands; the different indicator categories (i.e., facultative species, and obligate wetland species) are defined elsewhere in this glossary.

Wooded swamp - A wetland dominated by trees; a forested wetland.

Zone of influence - The area contiguous to a ditch, channel, or other drainage structure that is directly affected by it.

Appendix A
Selected Wetland References

I. WETLAND FIELD GUIDES

Burkhalter, A.P., L.M. Curtis, R.L. Lazor, M.L. Beach, and J.C. Hudson. 1973. AQUATIC WEED IDENTIFICATION AND CONTROL MANUAL. Bureau of Aquatic Plant Research and Control, Florida Department of Natural Resources, Tallahassee, FL. 100 pp.

Chabreck, R.H., and R.E. Condrey. 1979. COMMON VASCULAR PLANTS OF THE LOUISIANA MARSH. Louisiana State University Center for Wetland Resources, Baton Rouge, LA. Sea Grant Publ. No. LSU-T-79-003. 116 pp.

Clark, L.J. 1974. LEWIS CLARK'S FIELD GUIDE TO WILDFLOWERS OF MARSHES AND WATERWAYS IN THE PACIFIC NORTHWEST. Gray's Publishing, Ltd., Sidney, BC.

Eggers, S.D. and D.M. Reed. 1988. WETLAND PLANTS AND PLANT COMMUNITIES OF MINNESOTA AND WISCONSIN. US Army Corps of Engineers, St. Paul District, St. Paul, MN. 201 pp.

Eleutrius, L.N. 1980. AN ILLUSTRATED GUIDE TO TIDAL MARSH PLANTS OF MISSISSIPPI AND ADJACENT STATES. Mississippi-Alabama Sea Grant Consortium, Gulf Coast Research Laboratory, Ocean Springs, MS. Publ. No. MASGP-77-039. 130 pp.

Eliott, M.E., and E.M. Hall. 1977. WETLANDS AND WETLAND VEGETATION OF HAWAII. US Army Corps of Engineers, Pacific Ocean Division, Fort Shafter, HI. 344 pp.

Eyles, D.E., and J.L. Robertson. 1963. A GUIDE AND KEY TO THE AQUATIC PLANTS OF THE SOUTHEASTERN UNITED STATES. USDI, Fish and Wildlife Service, Bureau of Sport Fisheries and Wildlife, Washington, DC. Circular 158 (reprint of Public Health Bulletin 286 (1944)). 151 pp.

Fairbrothers, D.E., E.T. Moul, A.R. Essbach, D.N. Riemer, D.A. Schallock. 1979. AQUATIC VEGETATION OF NEW JERSEY. Extension Service, College of Agriculture, Rutgers-The State University, New Brunswick, NJ. Extension Bulletin No. 382. 107 pp.

Faber, P.M. 1982. COMMON WETLAND PLANTS OF COASTAL CALIFORNIA. Pickleweed Press, Mill Valley, CA. 110 pp.

Hotchkiss, N. 1964. PONDWEEDS AND PONDWEEDLIKE PLANTS OF EASTERN NORTH AMERICA. US Fish and Wildlife Service, Washington, DC. Circular 187. 30 pp.

Hotchkiss, N. 1965. BULRUSHES AND BULRUSHLIKE PLANTS OF EASTERN NORTH AMERICA. USDI, Fish and Wildlife Service, Washington, DC. Circular 221. 19 pp.

Hotchkiss, N. 1970. COMMON MARSH PLANTS OF THE UNITED STATES AND CANADA. US Fish and Wildlife Service, Washington, DC. Resources Publication No. 93.

Hotchkiss, N. 1972. COMMON MARSH, UNDERWATER AND FLOATING-LEAVED PLANTS OF THE UNITED STATES AND CANADA. Dover Publications, New York, NY.

Illinois Department of Conservation. 1988. A FIELD GUIDE TO THE WETLANDS OF ILLINOIS. State of Illinois. 240 pp.

Klussmann, W.G., F.G. Lowman, and J.T. Davis. 1974. COMMON AQUATIC PLANTS OF TEXAS. Texas Agricultural Extension Service and Texas A&M University System. Publ. No. B-1018. 16 pp.

Magee, D.W. 1981. FRESHWATER WETLANDS: A GUIDE TO COMMON INDICATOR PLANTS OF THE NORTHEAST. University of Massachusetts Press, Amherst, MA. 245 pp.

Matsumura, Y. 1955. THE TRUE AQUATIC VASCULAR PLANTS OF COLORADO. Colorado Agricultural Experiment Station, Colorado Ag. and Mech. College, Ft. Collins, CO. 130 pp.

McCormick, J. 1978. VEGETATION TYPICAL OF ALASKAN WETLANDS. Kenai River Review, US Army Corps of Engineers District, Alaska Corps of Engineers. 15 pp.

Nelson, E.N., and R.W. Couch. 1985. AQUATIC PLANTS OF OKLAHOMA. I: SUBMERSED, FLOATING-LEAVED, AND SELECTED EMERGENT MACROPHYTES. Oral Roberts University, Tulsa, OK. 111 pp.

Otto, N.E. 1980. AQUATIC PESTS ON IRRIGATION SYSTEMS, IDENTIFICATION GUIDE. (2nd. ed.). Department of the Interior, Water and Power Resources Service, Denver, CO. 90 pp.

Prescott, G.W. 1969. HOW TO KNOW THE AQUATIC PLANTS. Brown Co., Dubuque, IA. 171 pp.

Schlosser, D.W. 1986. A FIELD GUIDE TO VALUABLE UNDERWATER AQUATIC PLANTS OF THE GREAT LAKES. Michigan State University, East Lansing, MI. 32 pp.

Silberhorn, G.M. 1976. TIDAL WETLAND PLANTS OF VIRGINIA. Virginia Institute of Marine Sciences, Gloucester Point, VA. Educational Series No. 19. 86 pp.

Stemmermann, L. 1981. A GUIDE TO PACIFIC WETLAND PLANTS. US Army Corps of Engineers.

Taylor, J. 1977. A CATALOG OF VASCULAR AQUATIC AND WETLAND PLANTS THAT GROW IN OKLAHOMA. Southeastern Oklahoma State University Herbarium, Durant, OK. Pub. No. 1. 75 pp.

Tarver, D.P., J.A. Rodgers, M.J. Mahler, R.L. Lazor. 1978. AQUATIC AND WETLAND PLANTS OF FLORIDA. Bureau of Aquatic Plant Research and Control, Florida Department of Natural Resources, Tallahassee, FL. 127 pp.

Tiner, R.W. Jr. 1987. A FIELD GUIDE TO COASTAL WETLAND PLANTS OF THE NORTHEASTERN UNITED STATES. University of Massachusetts Press, Amherst, MA. 285 pp.

Tiner, R.W. Jr. 1988. FIELD GUIDE TO NONTIDAL WETLAND IDENTIFICATION. Maryland Department of Natural Resources, Annapolis, MD and US Fish and Wildlife Service, Newton Corner, MA. 283 pp. plus 198 color plates.

US Army Corps of Engineers. Undated. COMMON WETLAND PLANTS OF SOUTHWEST TEXAS. Galveston Corps of Engineers District, Galveston, TX.

US Army Corps of Engineers. 1977. WETLAND PLANTS OF THE NEW ORLEANS DISTRICT. New Orleans Corps of Engineers District, New Orleans, LA.

US Army Corps of Engineers. 1977. WETLAND PLANTS OF THE EASTERN UNITED STATES. North Atlantic Corps of Engineers Division, New York, NY. Publ. No. 200-1-1.

US Army Corps of Engineers. 1978. PRELIMINARY GUIDE TO WETLANDS OF THE GULF COASTAL PLAIN. US Army Engineer Waterways Experiment Station, Vicksburg, MS. Technical Report Y-78-5.

US Army Corps of Engineers. 1979. SUPPLEMENT TO WETLAND PLANTS OF THE EASTERN UNITED STATES. North Atlantic Division, New York, NY. NADP-200-1-1, Suppl. 1.

US Army Corps of Engineers. 1988. A GUIDE TO SELECTED FLORIDA WETLAND PLANTS AND COMMUNITIES. Jacksonville District, Jacksonville, FL. Publ. No. CESAOP 7745-2-1. 319 pp.

Weinmann, F., M. Boule, K. Brunner, J. Malek, and V. Yoshino. 1984. WETLAND PLANTS OF THE PACIFIC NORTHWEST. US Army Corps of Engineers, Seattle District, Seattle, WA. 85 pp.

Winterringer, G.S., and A.C. Lopinot. 1977. AQUATIC PLANTS OF ILLINOIS. Department of Registration and Education, Illinois State Museum Division and Department of Conservation, Division of Fisheries, Illinois State Museum, Springfield, IL. 142 pp.

II. WETLAND PLANT TAXONOMIC MANUALS AND CHECKLISTS

Beal, E.O. 1977. A MANUAL OF MARSH AND AQUATIC VASCULAR PLANTS OF NORTH CAROLINA WITH HABITAT DATA. North Carolina Agricultural Experiment Station, Raleigh, NC. 298 pp.

Beal, E.O., and J.W. Thieret. 1986. AQUATIC AND WETLAND PLANTS OF KENTUCKY. Kentucky Nature Preserves Commission. Soil and Technical Service Publ. No. 5. 315 pp.

Brooks, E., and L.A. Hauser. 1981. AQUATIC VASCULAR PLANTS OF KANSAS I: SUBMERGED AND FLOATING LEAVED PLANTS. State Biological Survey of Kansas, The University of Kansas, Lawrence, KS.

Crawford, V. 1981. WETLAND PLANTS OF KING COUNTY AND THE PUGET SOUND LOWLANDS. King County, WA. 80 pp.

Correll, D.S., and H.B. Correll. 1972. AQUATIC AND WETLAND PLANTS OF THE SOUTHWESTERN UNITED STATES. Environmental Protection Agency, Washington, DC. Publ. No. 16030 DNL 01/72. 1777 pp.

Correll, D.S., and H.B. Correll. 1975. AQUATIC AND WETLAND PLANTS OF SOUTHWESTERN UNITED STATES. VOLUMES 1 AND 2. Stanford University Press, Stanford, CA. Vol 1-856 pp, Vol. 2-1777 pp.

Fassett, N.C. 1975. A MANUAL OF AQUATIC PLANTS. University of Wisconsin Press, Madison, WI. 405 pp.

Godfrey, R.K. and J.W. Wooten. 1979. AQUATIC AND WETLAND PLANTS OF SOUTHEASTERN UNITED STATES. MONOCOTYLEDONS. University of Georgia Press, Athens, GA.

Godfrey, R.K. and J.W. Wooten. 1981. AQUATIC AND WETLAND PLANTS OF SOUTHEASTERN UNITED STATES. DICOTYLEDONS. University of Georgia Press, Athens, GA.

Hartog, C.D. 1970. THE SEA-GRASSES OF THE WORLD. North-Holland Publishing Company, Amsterdam. 275 pp.

Hermann, F.J. 1975. MANUAL OF THE RUSHES (*JUNCUS* SPP.) OF THE ROCKY MOUNTAINS AND COLORADO BASIN. USDA, Forest Service, Rocky Mountain Forest and Range Experiment Station, Fort Collins, CO. Gen. Tech. Rpt. RM-18. 107 pp.

Hotchkiss, N. 1950. CHECKLIST OF MARSH AND AQUATIC PLANTS OF THE UNITED STATES. USDI, Fish and Wildlife Service, Washington, DC. Wildlife Leaflet No. 210. 34 pp.

Jones, S.B. 1974. MISSISSIPPI FLORA. I. MONOCOTYLEDON FAMILIES WITH AQUATIC OR WETLAND SPECIES. *Gulf Research Reports* 4(3):357-379.

Jones, S.B. 1975. MISSISSIPPI FLORA. IV. DICOTYLEDON FAMILIES WITH AQUATIC OR WETLAND SPECIES. *Gulf Research Reports* 5(1):7-22.

Larson, G.E., and W.T. Barker. 1980. THE AQUATIC AND WETLAND VASCULAR PLANTS OF NORTH DAKOTA. North Dakota Water Resources Research Institute, North Dakota State University, Fargo, ND. Project No. 064 NDAK, Research Project Technical Completion Report. 453 pp.

Lindstrom, L.E. 1968. THE AQUATIC AND MARSH PLANTS OF THE GREAT PLAINS OF CENTRAL NORTH AMERICA. Ph.D. Dissertation. Kansas State University, Manhattan, KS. 247 pp.

Mason, H. L. 1957. FLORA OF THE MARSHES OF CALIFORNIA. University of California Press, CA. 897 pp.

Muenscher, W.C. 1972. AQUATIC PLANTS OF THE UNITED STATES. Cornell University Press, Ithaca, NY.

Reed, P.B., Jr. 1988. NATIONAL LIST OF PLANT SPECIES THAT OCCUR IN WETLANDS: NATIONAL SUMMARY. U.S. Fish and Wildlife Service, Washington, DC. Biol. Rpt. 88(24). 244 pp.

Robinson, T.W. 1958. PHREATOPHYTES. USDI, Geological Survey, Washington, DC. Water Supply Paper No. 1423. 84 pp.

Smeins, F.E. 1967. THE WETLAND VEGETATION OF THE RED RIVER VALLEY AND DRIFT PRAIRIE REGIONS OF MINNESOTA, NORTH DAKOTA, AND MANITOBA. Ph.D. Dissertation. University of Saskatchewan, CN. 226 pp.

Rowell, C.M. 1971. VASCULAR PLANTS OF PLAYA LAKES OF THE TEXAS PANHANDLE AND SOUTH PLAINS. *Southwestern Naturalist* 15(4):407-417.

Stewart, A.N., L.J. Dennis, and H.M. Gilkey. 1963. AQUATIC PLANTS OF THE PACIFIC NORTHWEST. Oregon State University Press, Corvallis, OR. 261 pp.

USDA. 1970. MANUAL OF THE CARICES OF THE ROCKY MOUNTAINS AND COLORADO BASIN. Agric. Handbook No. 374. Washington, DC.

III. OTHER FIELD GUIDES FOR PLANT IDENTIFICATION

Ajilvsgi, G. 1979. WILD FLOWERS OF THE BIG THICKET, EAST TEXAS AND WESTERN LOUISIANA. Texas A&M University Press, College Station, TX. 360 pp.

Belzer, T.J. 1984. ROADSIDE PLANTS OF SOUTHERN CALIFORNIA. Mountain Press Publishing Company, Missoula, MT. 158 pp.

Brown, C.A. 1972. WILD FLOWERS OF LOUISIANA AND ADJOINING STATES. Louisiana State University Press, Baton Rouge, LA. 247 pp.

Brown, L. 1976. WEEDS IN WINTER. Houghton Mifflin Co., Boston, MA.

Cobb, B. 1963. A FIELD GUIDE TO THE FERNS AND THEIR RELATED FAMILIES OF NORTH-EASTERN AND CENTRAL NORTH AMERICA. Houghton Mifflin Co., Boston, MA. 281 pp.

Courtenay, B. and J.H. Zimmerman. 1972. WILDFLOWERS AND WEEDS. Van Nostrand Reinhold Company, New York, NY. 144 pp.

Dawson, E.Y. 1966. SEASHORE PLANTS OF NORTHERN CALIFORNIA. University of California Press, Berkeley, CA. 103 pp.

Dawson, E.Y. 1966. SEASHORE PLANTS OF SOUTHERN CALIFORNIA. University of California Press, Berkeley, CA. 101 pp.

Dean, B.E., A. Mason, and J.L. Thomas. 1973. WILD FLOWERS OF ALABAMA AND ADJOINING STATES. University of Alabama Press, Tuscaloosa, AL. 230 pp.

Duncan, W.H., and L.E. Foote. 1975. WILDFLOWERS OF THE SOUTHEASTERN UNITED STATES. University of Georgia Press, Athens, GA. 296 pp.

Faber, P.M., and R.F. Holland. 1988. COMMON RIPARIAN PLANTS OF CALIFORNIA, A FIELD GUIDE FOR THE LAYMAN. Pickleweed Press, Mill Valley, CA. 140 pp.

Fleming, G., P. Genelle, and R.W. Long. 1976. WILD FLOWERS OF FLORIDA. Banyan Books, Inc., Miami, FL. 96 pp.

Grimm, W.C. 1957. THE BOOK OF SHRUBS. Bonanza Books, NY. 522 pp.

Grimm, W.C. 1970. HOME GUIDE TO TREES, SHRUBS, AND WILDFLOWERS. Bonanza Books, NY. 320 pp.

Harlow, W.H. 1941. FRUIT KEY AND TWIG KEY TO TREES AND SHRUBS. Dover Publications, New York, NY.

Harrar, E.S., and J.G. Harrar. 1962. GUIDE TO SOUTHERN TREES. Dover Publications, Inc., New York, NY. 709 pp.

Harrington, H.D. 1977. HOW TO IDENTIFY GRASSES AND GRASSLIKE PLANTS. The Swallow Press, Inc., Chicago. IL. 142 pp.

Heller, C.A. 1966. WILD EDIBLE AND POISONOUS PLANTS OF ALASKA. Cooperative Extension Service, University of Alaska. Publ. No. 28. 89 pp.

Horn, E.L. 1972. WILDFLOWERS OF THE PACIFIC CASCADES. The Touchtone Press, Beaverton, OR. 157 pp.

Hunter, C.G. 1984. WILDFLOWERS OF ARKANSAS. The Ozark Society Foundation, Little Rock, AR. 296 pp.

Jolley, R. 1988. A COMPREHENSIVE FIELD GUIDE: WILDFLOWERS OF THE COLUMBIA RIVER GORGE. Oregon Historical Society Press, Portland, OR. 331 pp.

Justice, W.S., and C.R. Bell. 1968. WILDFLOWERS OF NORTH CAROLINA. University of North Carolina Press, Chapel Hill, NC. 217 pp.

Knoble, E. 1977. FIELD GUIDE TO THE GRASSES, SEDGES, AND RUSHES OF THE UNITED STATES. (Reprint). Dover Publishing, Inc., NY. 83 pp.

Lamb, S.H. 1975. WOODY PLANTS OF THE SOUTHWEST: A FIELD GUIDE WITH DESCRIPTIVE TEXT. The Sunstone Press, Santa Fe, NM. 177 pp.

Little, E.L. 1985. THE AUDUBON SOCIETY FIELD GUIDE TO NORTH AMERICAN TREES: EASTERN REGION. Alfred A. Knopf, Inc., New York, NY.

Loughmiller, C., and L. Loughmiller. 1984. TEXAS WILDFLOWERS. University of Texas Press, Austin, TX. 271 pp.

Mathews, F.S. 1915. FIELD BOOK OF AMERICAN TREES AND SHRUBS. G.P. Putnam and Sons, NY. 537 pp.

Mathews, F.S. 1955. FIELD BOOK OF AMERICAN WILD FLOWERS. G.P. Putnam and Sons, New York, NY. 601 pp.

Mattoon, W.R. 1977. FOREST TREES OF FLORIDA. Tenth Edition. Florida Department of Agriculture and Consumer Services, Division of Forestry, Tallahassee, FL. 98 pp.

Moldenke, H.N. 1949. AMERICAN WILD FLOWERS. D. Van Nostrand Company, Inc., New York, NY. 543 pp.

Moyle, J.B. 1953. A FIELD KEY TO THE COMMON NON-WOODY FLOWERING PLANTS AND FERNS OF MINNESOTA. Burgess Publishing Co., Minneapolis, MN. 72 PP.

Muenscher, W.C. 1950. KEYS TO WOODY PLANTS. Cornell University Press, Ithaca, NY.

Munz, P.A. 1964. SHORE WILDFLOWERS OF CALIFORNIA, OREGON, AND WASHINGTON. University of California Press, CA.

Nelson, R.A. 1969. HANDBOOK OF ROCKY MOUNTAIN PLANTS. Dale Stuart King, Tuscon, AZ. 331 pp.

Newcomb, L. 1977. NEWCOMB'S WILDFLOWER GUIDE. Little, Brown and Co., Boston, MA.

Niehaus, T.F., and C.L. Ripper. 1976. A FIELD GUIDE TO PACIFIC STATES WILDFLOWERS. Houghton-Mifflin Company, Boston, MA. 432 pp.

Niehaus, T.F., J. Jousey, and J. McLean. 1984. A FIELD GUIDE TO SOUTHWESTERN AND TEXAS WILDFLOWERS. Houghton-Mifflin Company, Boston, MA. 449 pp.

Niering, W.A. and W.C. Olmstead. 1979. THE AUDUBON SOCIETY FIELD GUIDE TO NORTH AMERICAN WILDFLOWERS: EASTERN REGION. Alfred A. Knopf, Inc., New York, NY.

Petrides, G.A. 1958. A FIELD GUIDE TO THE TREES AND SHRUBS. Houghton Mifflin Co., Boston, MA.

Peterson, R.T. and M. McKenny. 1968. A FIELD GUIDE TO WILDFLOWERS OF NORTHEASTERN AND NORTH CENTRAL NORTH AMERICA. Houghton Mifflin Co., Boston, MA.

Rickett, H.W. 1979. WILD FLOWERS OF THE UNITED STATES. VOLUMES I-VI PLUS INDEX. The New York Botanical Garden, McGraw-Hill Book Company, New York, NY. Vol. I-559 pp., Vol II-688 pp., Vol III-553 pp, Vol IV-801 pp, Vol V-666 pp, Vol VI-784 pp, Index-152 pp.

Smith, E.C., and L.W. Durrell. 1944. SEDGES AND RUSHES OF COLORADO. Colorado Agricultural Experiment Station, Colorado State University, Ft. Collins, CO. Tech. Bull. 32. 63 pp.

Soil Conservation Service. 1972. NATIVE FLOWERS OF TEXAS. USDA, Temple, TX.

Stevenson, G.B. 1969. TREES OF EVERGLADES NATIONAL PARK AND THE FLORIDA KEYS. Everglades Natural History Association, FL. 32 pp.

Tharp, B.C. 1952. TEXAS RANGE GRASSES. University of Texas Press, Austin, TX. 125 pp.

Thomas, J.H., and D.R. Parnell. 1974. NATIVE SHRUBS OF THE SIERRA NEVADA. University of California Press, Berkeley, CA. 127 pp.

Trelease, W. 1931. WINTER BOTANY. Dover Publications, New York, NY.

Van Bruggen, T. 1983. WILDFLOWERS, GRASSES AND OTHER PLANTS OF THE NORTHERN GREAT PLAINS AND BLACK HILLS. University of South Dakota, Vermillion, SD. 96 pp.

Vance, F., J. Jousey, and J. McLean. 1984. WILDFLOWERS OF THE NORTHERN GREAT PLAINS. University of Minnesota Press, Minneapolis, MN. 336 pp.

Warnock, B.H. 1970. WILDFLOWERS OF THE BIG BEND COUNTRY, TEXAS. Sul Ross State University, Alpine, TX. 156 pp.

Warnock, B.H. 1974. WILDFLOWERS OF THE GUADALUPE MOUNTAINS AND THE SAND DUNE COUNTRY, Texas. Sul Ross State University, Alpine, TX.

Warnock, B.H. 1977. WILDFLOWERS OF THE DAVIS MOUNTAINS AND MARATHON BASIN, TEXAS. Sul Ross State University, Alpine, TX. 274 pp.

Wharton, M.E., and R.W. Barbour. 1971. A GUIDE TO THE WILDFLOWERS AND FERNS OF KENTUCKY. University Press of Kentucky, Lexington, KY. 344 pp.

Wherry, E.T. 1964. THE SOUTHERN FERN GUIDE. Doubleday and Company, Inc., Garden City, NY. 349 pp.

White, H.A. 1974. ALASKA-YUKON WILDFLOWERS GUIDE. Alaska-Northwest Publishing Company, Anchorage, AK. 218 pp.

Wiedemann, A.M., L.J. Dennis, and F.H. Smith. 1974. PLANTS OF THE OREGON COASTAL DUNES. Oregon State University, Corvallis, OR. 117 pp.

IV. OTHER PLANT TAXONOMIC MANUALS, CHECKLISTS, AND ATLASES

Abrams, L. 1968. ILLUSTRATED FLORA OF THE PACIFIC STATES. VOLUMES 1-4. Stanford University Press, Stanford, CA. Vol. 1-538 pp; Vol 2-635 pp; Vol. 3-866 pp; Vol. 4-732 pp.

Ahmadjian, V. 1979. FLOWERING PLANTS OF MASSACHUSETTS. University of Massachusetts Press, Amherst, MA. 582 pp.

Allen, C.M. 1980. GRASSES OF LOUISIANA. University of Southwestern Louisiana, Lafayette, LA. 358 pp.

Barbour, M.G. and J. Major. 1977. TERRESTRIAL VEGETATION OF CALIFORNIA. John Wiley and Sons, New York, NY. 1002 pp.

Barkley, T.M. 1968. A MANUAL OF THE FLOWERING PLANTS OF KANSAS. Kansas State University Endowment Association, Manhattan KS. 402 pp.

Barkley, T.M. 1977. ATLAS OF THE FLORA OF THE GREAT PLAINS. The Iowa State University Press, Ames, IA. 600 pp.

Batson, W.T. 1977. GENERA OF THE EASTERN PLANTS: A GUIDE TO THE GENERA OF NATIVE AND COMMONLY INTRODUCED FERNS AND SEED PLANTS OF EASTERN NORTH AMERICA. John Wiley and Sons, NY.

Batson, W.T. 1982. GENERA OF THE WESTERN PLANTS. The State Printing Company, Columbia, SC. 207 pp.

Benson, L., and R.A. Darrow. 1981. TREES AND SHRUBS OF THE SOUTHWESTERN DESERTS. University of Arizona Press, Tuscon, AZ. 416 pp.

Billington, C. 1948. SHRUBS OF MICHIGAN. Cranbrook Institute of Science, Bloomfield Hills, MI. Bulletin 20. 339 pp.

Billington, C. 1952. FERNS OF MICHIGAN. Cranbrook Institute of Science, The Cranbrook Press, Bloomfield Hills, MI. Bulletin 32. 240 pp.

Booth, W.E. 1972. GRASSES OF MONTANA. Montana State University, Bozeman, MT. 64 pp.

Booth, W.E., and J.C. Wright. 1967. FLORA OF MONTANA. PART 2. Montana State University, Bozeman, MT. 305 pp.

Braun, E.L. 1946. AN ANNOTATED CATALOG OF SPERMATOPHYTES OF KENTUCKY. John S. Swift Co., Inc., Cincinnati, OH. 161 pp.

Braun, E.L. 1967. THE VASCULAR FLORA OF OHIO. VOLUME I. THE MONOCOTYLEDONEAE. Ohio State University Press, Columbus, OH. 464 pp.

Britton, N.L., and H.A. Brown. 1970. AN ILLUSTRATED FLORA OF THE NORTHERN UNITED STATES AND CANADA, VOLUMES 1,2, AND 3. Dover Publications, Inc., New York, NY. Vol. 1-680 pp, Vol 2-735 pp, Vol 3-637 pp.

Britton, N.L., and W. Wilson. 1924. BOTANY OF PUERTO RICO AND THE VIRGIN ISLANDS. Scientific Survey of Puerto Rico and the Virgin Islands Vol. 5, 6 Part 1, Descriptive Flora-Spermatophyta. New York Academy of Sciences, New York, NY.

Brooks, R.E. 1986. VASCULAR PLANTS OF KANSAS: A CHECKLIST. Kansas Biological Survey, The University of Kansas Press, Lawrence, KS. 129 pp.

Brown, M.L. and R.G. Brown. 1972. WOODY PLANTS OF MARYLAND. Port City Press, Baltimore, MD.

Brown, M.L. and R.G. Brown. 1984. HERBACEOUS PLANTS OF MARYLAND. Port City Press, Baltimore, MD.

Clewell, A.F. 1985. GUIDE TO THE VASCULAR PLANTS OF THE FLORIDA PANHANDLE. University Presses of Florida, Tallahassee, FL. 605 pp.

Coker, W.C., and H.R. Totten. TREES OF THE SOUTHEASTERN STATES. University of North Carolina Press, Chapel Hill, NC. 417 pp.

Correll, D.S., and M.C. Johnston. 1979. MANUAL OF THE VASCULAR PLANTS OF TEXAS. University of Texas, Dallas, TX. 1881 pp.

Crampton, B. 1974. GRASSES IN CALIFORNIA. University of California Press, Berkeley, CA. 178 pp.

Cronquist, A.C. 1980. VASCULAR FLORA OF THE SOUTHEASTERN UNITED STATES. VOLUME I. ASTERACEAE. University of North Carolina Press, Chapel Hill, NC. 261 pp.

Cronquist, A., A.H. Holmgren, N.H. Holmgren and J.L. Reveal. 1972. INTERMOUNTAIN FLORA - VASCULAR PLANTS OF THE INTERMOUNTAIN WEST, USA. Hafner Publishing Company, NY. (Two Vols.). 584 pp.

Davis, R.J. 1952. FLORA OF IDAHO. William C. Brown Company, Dubuque, IA. 828 pp.

Dean, C.C. 1970. FLORA OF INDIANA. Lehre, J.P. Cramer, NY. 1236 pp.

Dittmer, H.J., E.F. Castetter, and O.M. Clark. 1954. THE FERNS AND FERN ALLIES OF NEW MEXICO. University of New Mexico Press, Albuquerque, NM. 139 pp.

Dorn, R.D. 1977. MANUAL OF THE VASCULAR PLANTS OF WYOMING. 2 VOLUMES. Garland Publishing, Inc., NY. Vol. 1-538 pp; Vol. II-960 pp.

Duncan, W.H. 1967. WOODY VINES OF THE SOUTHEASTERN UNITED STATES. University of Georgia Press, Athens, GA. 76 pp.

Fernald, M.L. 1970. GRAY'S MANUAL OF BOTANY. D. Van Nostrand Co., New York, NY.

Fowells, H.A. 1965. SILVICS OF FOREST TREES OF THE UNITED STATES. USDA, Agriculture Handbook No. 271. Washington, DC. 762 pp.

Gilkey, H.M., and L.J. Dennis. 1967. HANDBOOK OF NORTHWESTERN PLANTS. Oregon State University Bookstores, Inc., Corvallis, OR. 505 pp.

Gleason, H.A. 1952. THE NEW BRITTON AND BROWN ILLUSTRATED FLORA OF THE NORTHEASTERN UNITED STATES AND ADJACENT CANADA. Three Vols. 3rd. edition. Hafner Press, New York, NY. Vol I-482 pp; Vol II-655 pp; Vol. III-595 pp.

Gleason, H.A. and A. Cronquist. 1963. MANUAL OF VASCULAR PLANTS OF NORTHEASTERN UNITED STATES AND ADJACENT CANADA. D. Van Nostrand Co., New York, NY.

Gould, F.W. 1975. THE GRASSES OF TEXAS. Texas A&M University Press, College Station, TX. 653 pp.

Gould, F.W. 1975. TEXAS PLANTS - A CHECKLIST AND ECOLOGICAL SUMMARY. Texas A&M University System, The Texas Agricultural Experiment System, College Station, TX. 121 pp.

Gould, F.W., and T.W. Box. 1965. GRASSES OF THE TEXAS COASTAL BEND (CALHOUN, RE FUGIO, ARANSAS, SAN PATRICIO, AND NORTHERN KLEBERG COUNTIES). Texas A&M University Press, College Station, TX. 189 pp.

Gould, F.W. 1977. GRASSES OF SOUTHWESTERN UNITED STATES. University of Arizona Press Tucson, AZ. 352 pp.

Great Plains Flora Association. 1986. FLORA OF THE GREAT PLAINS. University of Kansas Press Lawrence, KS. 1392 pp.

Grillos, S.J. 1966. FERNS AND FERN ALLIES OF CALIFORNIA. University of California Press Berkeley, CA. 104 pp.

Hahn, B.E. 1977. FLORA OF MONTANA: CONIFERS AND MONOCOTS. Montana State University Bozeman, MT.

Harlow, W.M. 1957. TREES OF THE EASTERN AND CENTRAL UNITED STATES AND CANADA Dover Publications, Inc. New York, NY. 288 pp.

Harrington, H.D. 1964. MANUAL OF THE PLANTS OF COLORADO. Swallow Press, Inc., Chicago IL. 666 pp.

Harrington, H.D. 1979. MANUAL OF THE PLANTS OF COLORADO. Sage Books, Denver, CO (2nd. edition).

Hermann, F.J. 1970. MANUAL OF THE CARICES OF THE ROCKY MOUNTAINS AND COLORA- DO BASIN. USDA, Forest Service, Washington, DC. Agriculture Handbook No. 374. 397 pp.

Hitchcock, A.S. 1971. MANUAL OF THE GRASSES OF THE UNITED STATES. Dover Publications New York, NY. (Two Vols.).

Hitchcock, A.S. and A. Cronquist. 1973. FLORA OF THE PACIFIC NORTHWEST. University of Washington Press, Seattle, WA.

Hitchcock, A.S., A.C. Cronquist, M. Ownbey, and J.W. Thompson. 1977. VASCULAR PLANTS OF THE PACIFIC NORTHWEST. Vols. 1-5. University of Washington Press, Seattle, WA. Vol 1-914 pp, Vol 2-597 pp, Vol 3-614 pp, Vol. 4-510 pp, Vol. 5-343 pp.

Hulten, E. 1960. FLORA OF THE ALEUTIAN ISLANDS (SECOND EDITION). Hafner Publishing Company, New York, NY. 460 pp.

Hulten, E. 1868. FLORA OF ALASKA AND NEIGHBORING TERRITORIES: A MANUAL OF THE VASCULAR PLANTS. Stanford University Press, Stanford, CA. 1008 pp.

Jepson, W.L. 1975. A MANUAL OF THE FLOWERING PLANTS OF CALIFORNIA. University of California Press, Berkeley, CA. 1238 pp.

Jones, F.B. 1975. FLORA OF THE TEXAS COASTAL BEND. Mission Press, Corpus Christi, TX. 262 pp.

Jones, G.H. 1963. FLORA OF ILLINOIS. *American Midland Naturalist* Monograph No. 7. University of Notre Dame Press, Notre Dame, IN. 401 pp.

Jones, S.B. 1969. THE PTERIDOPHYTES OF MISSISSIPPI. *Sida* 3(6):359-364.

Jones, S.B. 1974. MISSISSIPPI FLORA. II. DISTRIBUTION AND IDENTIFICATION OF THE ONAGRACEAE. *Castanea* 39(4):370-379.

Jones, S.B. 1974. MISSISSIPPI FLORA. VI. MISCELLANEOUS FAMILIES. *Castanea* 41(3): 189-212.

Jones, S.B. 1975. MISSISSIPPI FLORA. III. DISTRIBUTION AND IDENTIFICATION OF THE BRASSICACEAE. *Castanea* 40(3):238-252.

Jones, S.B. 1976. MISSISSIPPI FLORA. V. THE MINT FAMILY. *Castanea* 41(1):41-58.

Jones, S.B., and N.C. Coile. 1979. LIST OF GEORGIA PLANTS IN THE UNIVERSITY OF GEORGIA HERBARIUM. Herbarium, Department of Botany, University of Georgia, Athens, GA. 53 pp.

Kartesz, J.T., and R. Kartesz. 1980. A SYNONYMIZED CHECKLIST OF THE VASCULAR FLORA OF THE UNITED STATES, CANADA, AND GREENLAND. The University of North Carolina Press, Chapel Hill, NC. 498 pp.

Kearney, T.H. and R.H. Peebles. 1960. ARIZONA FLORA. University of California Press, Berkeley, CA. (2nd. edition).

Kurz, H., and R.K. Godfrey. 1962. TREES OF NORTHERN FLORIDA. University of Florida Press, Gainesville, FL. 311 pp.

Lakela. O. 1965. FLORA OF NORTHEAST MINNESOTA. University of Minnesota Press, Minneapolis, MN. 541 pp.

Lakela, O., and R.W. Long. 1976. FERNS OF FLORIDA. Banyon Books, Miami, FL. 178 pp.

Little, E.L. 1971. ATLAS OF UNITED STATES TRESS, VOLUME, I. CONIFERS AND IMPORTANT HARDWOODS. USDA, Forest Service, Washington, DC. Miscellaneous Publ. No. 1146. 9 pp, 200 maps.

Little, E.L. 1976. ATLAS OF UNITED STATES TREES. VOLUME III. MINOR WESTERN HARDWOODS. USDA, Forest Service, Washington, D.C. Miscellaneous Publ. No. 1314. 13 pp., 210 maps.

Little, E.L. 1976. SOUTHWESTERN TREES. USDA, Forest Service, Washington, DC. Agric. Handbook No. 9. 109 pp.

Little, E.L. 1978. ATLAS OF UNITED STATES TREES. VOLUME 5. FLORIDA. USDA, Forest Service, Washington, DC. Miscellaneous Publ. No. 1361. 256 pp.

Little, E.L. 1979. CHECKLIST OF UNITED STATES TREES (NATIVE AND NATURALIZED). USDA, Forest Service, Washington, DC. Agricultural Handbook No. 541. 375 pp.

Little, E.L., R.D. Woodbury, and F.H. Wadsworth. 1974. TREES OF PUERTO RICO AND THE VIRGIN ISLANDS: SECOND VOLUME. USDA, Forest Service, Washington, DC. Agric. Handbook No. 449. 1024 pp.

Lloyd, R.M., and R.S. Mitchell. 1973. A FLORA OF THE WHITE MOUNTAINS, CALIFORNIA AND NEVADA. University of California Press, Berkeley, CA. 202 pp.

Looman, J. 1982. PRAIRIE GRASSES, IDENTIFIED AND DESCRIBED BY VEGETATIVE CHARACTERISTICS. Agriculture Canada Research Station, Swift Current, SK. Publ. 1413. 244 pp.

Long, R.W. and O. Lakela. 1976. A FLORA OF TROPICAL FLORIDA. Banyan Books, Miami, FL.

Lowe, E.N. 1921. PLANTS OF MISSISSIPPI. Mississippi State Geological Survey, MS. Bulletin No. 17. 295 pp.

Mackenzie, K.K. 1940. NORTH AMERICAN CARICEAE, VOLS. I-II. New York Botanical Garden, NY. 543 pp.

Martin, W.C., and C.R. Hutchins. 1981. A FLORA OF NEW MEXICO. J. Cramer, Braunchweig, West Germany. 2591 pp.

Massey, A.B. 1961. VIRGINIA FLORA. Virginia Agricultural Experiment Station, Blacksburg, VA. Tech. Bull. No. 155. 258 pp.

McDougall, W.B. 1973. SEED PLANTS OF NORTHERN ARIZONA. Museum of Northern Arizona, Flagstaff, AZ. 594 pp.

McGregor, R.L. 1986. FLORA OF THE GREAT PLAINS. University of Kansas Press, Lawrence, KS. 1392 pp.

McMinn, H.E. 1974. AN ILLUSTRATED MANUAL OF CALIFORNIA SHRUBS. University of California Press, Berkeley, CA. 663 pp.

Mohlenbrock, R.H. 1967. THE ILLUSTRATED FLORA OF ILLINOIS. Multiple Vols. Southern Illinois University Press, Carbondale, IL.

Mohlenbrock, R.H. 1975. GUIDE TO THE VASCULAR FLORA OF ILLINOIS. Southern Illinois University Press, Carbondale, IL. 494 pp.

Mohlenbrook, R.H., and D.M. Ladd. 1978. DISTRIBUTION OF ILLINOIS VASCULAR PLANTS. Southern Illinois University Press, Carbondale and Edwardsville, IL. 281 pp.

Mohr, C. 1901. PLANT LIFE OF ALABAMA. Alabama Edition, The Brown Printing Company, Montgomery, AL. 519 pp.

Morley, T. 1969. SPRING FLORA OF MINNESOTA, INCLUDING COMMON CULTIVATED PLANTS. The University of Minnesota Press, Minneapolis, MN. 283 pp.

Munz, P.A. 1974. A FLORA OF SOUTHERN CALIFORNIA. University of California Press, Berkeley, CA. 1086 PP.

Munz, P.A. and D.D. Keck. 1959. A CALIFORNIA FLORA. University of California Press, Berkeley, CA.

Norton, J.B.S., and R.G. Brown. 1946. A CATALOG OF THE VASCULAR PLANTS OF MARYLAND. University of Maryland Agricultural Experiment Station, College Park, MD.

Oklahoma State Department of Agriculture (Forestry Division). 1981. FOREST TREES OF OKLAHOMA: HOW TO KNOW THEM. Revised by E.L. Little, Jr. Oklahoma City, OK. Publ. No. 1, Rev. Ed. No. 12. 204 pp.

Peattie, D.C. 1930. FLORA OF THE INDIANA DUNES. Field Museum of Natural History, Chicago, IL. 405 pp.

Peck, M.E. 1961. A MANUAL OF THE HIGHER PLANTS OF OREGON. Oregon State University Press, Portland, OR. 936 pp.

Petersen, N.F. 1912. FLORA OF NEBRASKA. (2nd. edition). N.F. Petersen, Plainview, NE. 217 pp.

Porter, C.L. 1972. A FLORA OF WYOMING. Parts 1,2,5,6,7,8. Agricultural Experiment Station, University of Wyoming, Laramie, WY. Bulletin 402, Bulletin 404, Research Journal 14, Research Journal 20, Research Journal 64, Research Journal 65. Part 1-39 pp; Part 2-16 pp; Part 5-37 pp; Part 6-63 pp; Part 7-49 pp; Part 8-40 pp.

Pohl, R.W. 1966. THE GRASSES OF IOWA. *Iowa State Journal of Science* 40(4):341-566. Iowa State University Press, Ames, IA.

Preston, J. 1976. NORTH AMERICAN TREES. The Iowa State University Press, Ames, IA. 399 pp.

Preston, R.J., and V.G. Wright. 1982. IDENTIFICATION OF SOUTHEASTERN TREES IN WINTER. North Carolina Agricultural Extension Service, Raleigh, NC. 113 pp.

Putnam, J.A., and H. Bull. 1932. THE TREES OF THE BOTTOMLANDS OF THE MISSISSIPPI RIVER DELTA REGION. USDA, Forest Service, Southern Forest Experiment Station, New Orleans, LA. Occasional Paper No. 27. 207 pp.

Radford, A.E., H.E. Ahles, and C.R. Bell. 1968. MANUAL OF THE VASCULAR FLORA OF THE CAROLINAS. University of North Carolina Press, Chapel Hill, NC.

Reed, C. 1953. THE FERNS AND FERN ALLIES OF MARYLAND AND DELAWARE, INCLUDING DISTRICT OF COLUMBIA. Reed Herbarium, Baltimore, MD.

Rock, J.F. 1974. THE INDIGENOUS TREES OF THE HAWAIIAN ISLANDS. Pacific Tropical Botanical Garden, Lawai, Kauai, HA. 548 pp.

Rotar, P.P. 1968. GRASSES OF HAWAII. University of Hawaii Press, Honolulu, HA. 355 pp.

Rydberg, P.A. 1965. FLORA OF THE PRAIRIES AND PLAINS OF CENTRAL NORTH AMERICA. Hafner Publishing Company, New York, NY. Facsimile of the Edition of 1932. 969 pp.

Rydberg, P.A. 1969. FLORA OF THE ROCKY MOUNTAINS AND ADJACENT PLAINS. Hafner Publishing Company, New York, NY. 1143 pp.

Sargent, C.S. 1965. TREES OF NORTH AMERICA. Dover Publications, New York, NY. (Two Vols.).

Scoggan, H.J. 1978. THE FLORA OF CANADA. National Museum of Natural Sciences Publications in Botany, National Museums of Canada, Ottawa, Canada. Publ. No. 7. 1711 pp.

Seymour, F.C. 1969. THE FLORA OF VERMONT. Agricultural Experiment Station, University of Vermont, Burlington, VT. Bulletin No. 660. 393 pp.

Shreve, F., and I.L. Wiggins. 1964. VEGETATION AND FLORA OF THE SONORAN DESERT, VOLUME 1 AND VOLUME 2. Stanford University Press, Stanford, CA. Vol. 1-840 pp, Vol. 2-1740 pp.

Small, J.K. 1918. FERNS OF TROPICAL FLORIDA. Published by the Author, NY. 82 pp.

Small, J.K. 1933. MANUAL OF THE SOUTHEASTERN FLORA. The University of North Carolina Press, Chapel Hill, NC.

Smith, H.V. 1966. MICHIGAN WILDFLOWERS. Cranbrook Institute of Science, The Cranbrook Press, Bloomfield Hills, MI. Bulletin 42 (Revised).

Smith, E.B. 1978. AN ATLAS AND ANNOTATED LIST OF THE VASCULAR PLANTS OF ARKANSAS. University of Arkansas at Fayetteville, Fayetteville, AR. 562 pp.

Stephens, H.A. 1973. WOODY PLANTS OF THE NORTH CENTRAL PLAINS. University Press of Kansas, Lawrence, KS. 530 pp.

Stephens, H.A. 1969. TREES, SHRUBS, AND WOODY VINES IN KANSAS. Regents Press of Kansas, Lawrence, KS. 250 pp.

Stevens, O.A. 1963. HANDBOOK OF NORTH DAKOTA PLANTS. North Dakota Institute for Regional Studies, Fargo, ND. 324 pp.

Steyermark, J.A. 1963. FLORA OF MISSOURI. The Iowa State University Press, Ames, IA.

St. John, H. 1963. FLORA OF SOUTHWEST WASHINGTON. Outdoor Pictures, Escondido, CA. 583 pp.

St. John, H. 1973. LIST AND SUMMARY OF FLOWERING PLANTS IN THE HAWAIIAN ISLANDS. Pacific Tropical Botanical Garden, Memoir No. 1, Lawai, Kauai, Hawaii. 519 pp.

Strausbaugh, P.D. and E.L. Core. 1977. FLORA OF WEST VIRGINIA. 4 Vols. West Virginia University Books, Morgantown, WV. Bulletin, Series 70: 7-2. 1079 pp.

Stubbendieck, J., S.L. Hatch, and K.J. Kjar. 1982. NORTH AMERICAN RANGE PLANTS. University of Nebraska Press, Lincoln, NE. 464 pp.

Swink, F., and G. Wilhelm. 1979. PLANTS OF THE CHICAGO REGION. The Morton Arboretum, Lisle, IL. 922 pp.

Tatnall, R.R. 1946. FLORA OF DELAWARE AND THE EASTERN SHORE. Society of Natural History of Delaware, Intelligencer Printing Company, Lancaster, PA. 291 pp.

Thomson, O.S. 1976. SPRING FLORA OF WISCONSIN. University of Wisconsin Press, Madison, WI. 413 pp.

Thorne, R.F. 1954. THE VASCULAR PLANTS OF SOUTHWESTERN GEORGIA. *American Midland Naturalist* 52(2): 257-327.

Tidestrom, I. 1969. FLORA OF UTAH AND NEVADA. Reprints of US-Floras, Volume 3, Velag Von J. Cramer, S-H Service Agency, Inc., New York, NY. 665 pp.

U.S.D.A. Soil Conservation Service. 1982. NATIONAL LIST OF SCIENTIFIC PLANT NAMES. VOL. 1. LIST OF PLANT NAMES. VOL. 2. SYNONYMY. Washington, DC.

Van Bruggen, T. 1985. THE VASCULAR PLANTS OF SOUTH DAKOTA (2ND ED.). Iowa State University Press, Ames, IA. 476 pp.

Viereck, L.A. 1972. ALASKA TREES AND SHRUBS. USDA, Washington, DC. Agric. Handbook No. 410. 265 pp.

Vines, R.A. 1976. TREES, SHRUBS, AND WOODY VINES OF THE SOUTHWEST. University of Texas Press, Austin, TX. 1104 pp.

Voss, E. 1972. MICHIGAN FLORA. PART I. GYMNOSPERMS AND MONOCOTYLEDONS. Cranbrook Institute of Science, Bloomfield Hills, MI. 488 pp.

Voss, E. 1985. MICHIGAN FLORA. PART II. DICOTYLEDONS. Cranbrook Institute of Science, Bloomfield Hills, MI. 724 pp.

Wagner, W.L., and E.F. Aldon. 1978. MANUAL OF THE SALTBUSHES (*ATRIPLEX* SPP.) IN NEW MEXICO. USDA, Forest Service, Rocky Mountain Forest and Range Experiment Station, Ft. Collins, CO. General Technical Report RM-57. 50 pp.

Waterfall, U.T. 1979. KEYS TO THE FLORA OF OKLAHOMA. Oklahoma State University, Stillwater, OK. 246 pp.

Weber, W.A. 1976. ROCKY MOUNTAIN FLORA. Colorado Associated University Press, Boulder, CO. 479 pp.

Weber, W.A. 1987. COLORADO FLORA: WESTERN SLOPE. Colorado Associated University Press, Boulder, CO. 530 pp.

Weishaupt, C.G. 1960. VASCULAR PLANTS OF OHIO. Ohio State University Press, Columbus, OH. 307 pp.

Welsh, S.L. 1973. UTAH PLANTS. Brigham Young University Press, Provo, UT. 474 pp.

Welsh, S.L. 1974. ANDERSON'S FLORA OF ALASKA AND ADJACENT PARTS OF CANADA. Brigham Young University Press, UT. 724 pp.

West, E., and L.E. Arnold. 1950. THE NATIVES TREES OF FLORIDA. Fourth Printing. University of Florida Press, Gainesville, FL. 212 pp.

Wherry, T.E., J.M. Fogg, and H.A. Wahl. 1979. ATLAS OF THE FLORA OF PENNSYLVANIA. The Morris Arboretum, University of Pennsylvania, Philadelphia, PA. 390 pp.

Wiegand, K.M., and A.J. Eames. 1926. THE FLORA OF THE CAYUGA LAKE BASIN, NEW YORK. Cornell University Agricultural Experiment Station, Cornell University Press, Ithaca, NY. Memoir No. 92. 491 pp.

Wiggins, I.L., and J.H. Thomas. 1962. A FLORA OF THE ALASKAN ARCTIC SLOPE. Arctic Institute of North America, University of Toronto Press, Toronto, Canada. Spec. Publ. No. 4. 425 pp.

Wooton, E.O., and P.C. Standley. 1972. FLORA OF NEW MEXICO. Reprints of U.S. - Floras, Vol. 7. Stechert-Hafner Service Agency, Inc., New York, NY. 794 pp.

Wunderlin, R.P. 1982. GUIDE TO THE VASCULAR PLANTS OF CENTRAL FLORIDA. A University of South Florida Book, University Presses of Florida, Tampa. FL. 472 pp.

V. HYDRIC SOILS PUBLICATIONS

Bouma, J. 1983. HYDROLOGY AND SOIL GENESIS OF SOILS WITH AQUIC MOISTURE REGIMES. In: L.P. Wilding, N.E. Smeck, and G.F. Hall (editors), PEDOGENESIS AND SOIL TAXONOMY. I. CONCEPTS AND INTERACTIONS. Elsevier Science Publishers, B.V. Amsterdam. pp. 253-281.

Diers, R., and J.L. Anderson. 1984. PART I. DEVELOPMENT OF SOIL MOTTLING. *Soil Survey Horizons* (Winter): 9-12.

Edmonds, W.J., G.M. Silberhorn, P.R. Cobb, G.P. Peacock, Jr., N.A. McLoda, and D.W. Smith. 1985. CLASSIFICATION AND FLORAL RELATIONSHIPS OF SEASIDE SALT MARSH SOILS IN ACCOMACK AND NORTHAMPTON COUNTIES, VIRGINIA. Virginia Agricultural Experiment Station, VA. Bull. 85-8.

International Rice Research Institute. 1985. WETLAND SOILS: CHARACTERIZATION, CLASSIFICATION AND UTILIZATION. Manila, Philippines.

Lytle, S.A., and B.N. Driskell. 1954. PHYSICAL AND CHEMICAL CHARACTERISTICS OF THE PEATS, MUCKS AND CLAYS OF THE COASTAL MARSH AREA OF ST. MARY PARISH, LOUISIANA. Louisiana Agricultural Experiment Station. Bull. No. 484. 37 pp.

Phillips, J. 1970. WISCONSIN'S WETLAND SOILS, A REVIEW. Wisconsin Department of Natural Resources, Madison, WI. Res. Rpt. 57. 22 pp.

Ponnamperuma, F.N. 1972. THE CHEMISTRY OF SUBMERGED SOILS. *Advances in Agronomy* 24: 29-96.

Soil Survey Staff. 1988. KEYS TO SOIL TAXONOMY (FOURTH PRINTING). Cornell University, Ithaca, NY. SMSS Technical Monograph No. 6.

Tiner, R.W. Jr. and P.L.M. Veneman. 1987. HYDRIC SOILS OF NEW ENGLAND. University of Massachusetts Cooperative Extension, Amherst, MA. Bulletin C-183.

USDA, Soil Conservation Service. 1982. HYDRIC SOILS OF THE UNITED STATES. Washington, DC. National Bulletin No. 430-2-7. (January 4, 1982).

USDA, Soil Conservation Service. 1987. HYDRIC SOILS OF THE UNITED STATES. 1987. In cooperation with the National Technical Committee for Hydric Soils. USDA-SCS, Washington, DC.

Veneman, P.L.M., M.J. Vepraskas, and J. Bouma. 1976. THE PHYSICAL SIGNIFICANCE OF SOIL MOTTLING IN A WISCONSIN TOPOSEQUENCE. *Geoderma* 15: 103-118.

VI. OTHER SOILS MANUALS

Black, C.A. 1968. SOIL - PLANT RELATIONSHIPS. John Wiley & Sons, Inc., New York, NY.

Birkehead, P.W. 1984. SOILS AND GEOMORPHOLOGY. Oxford University Press, New York, NY. 372 pp.

Brady, Nyle C. 1974. THE NATURE AND PROPERTIES OF SOILS. MacMillan Publishing Co., Inc. 639 pp.

Buckman, H.O., and N.C. Brady. 1969. THE NATURE AND PROPERTIES OF SOILS. Macmillian Publishing Company, Ontario, Canada.

Buol, S.W., F.D. Hole, and R.J. McCracken. 1980. SOIL GENESIS AND CLASSIFICATION. The Iowa State University Press, Ames, IA. 406 pp.

Kollmorgen Corporation. 1975. MUNSELL SOIL COLOR CHARTS. Macbeth Division of Kollmorgen Corporation, Baltimore, MD.

Lytle, S.A. 1968. THE MORPHOLOGICAL CHARACTERISTICS AND RELIEF RELATIONSHIPS OF REPRESENTATIVE SOILS IN LOUISIANA. Louisiana Agricultural Experiment Station. Bull. No. 631. 23 pp.

Richards, L.A. 1954. DIAGNOSIS AND IMPROVEMENT OF SALINE AND ALKALI SOILS. USDA, Washington, DC. Agriculture Handbook No. 60. 196 pp. Reprinted Aug., 1969.

USDA, Soil Conservation Service. 1975. SOIL TAXONOMY. A BASIC SYSTEM OF SOIL CLASSIFICATION FOR MAKING AND INTERPRETING SOIL SURVEYS. U.S. Government Printing Office, Washington, DC. Agriculture Handbook No. 436. 754 pp.

USDA, Soil Conservation Service. 1983. NATIONAL SOILS HANDBOOK. Department of Agriculture, Washington, DC.

USDA, Soil Conservation Service. 1984. SOIL SURVEY MANUAL. Department of Agriculture, Washington, DC.

USDA, Soil Conservation Service. 1987. HYDRIC SOILS OF THE UNITED STATES. Washington, DC.

USDA, Soil Survey Staff. 1972. SOIL SERIES OF THE UNITED STATES, PUERTO RICO, AND THE VIRGIN ISLANDS: THEIR TAXONOMIC CLASSIFICATION. Department of Agriculture, Washington, DC.

USDA, Soil Survey Staff. 1951. SOIL SURVEY MANUAL. U.S. Government Printing Office, Washington, DC. Handbook No. 18. 502 pp.

VII. PLANT-SOIL STUDY REPORTS

Allen, S.D., F.C. Golet, A.F. Davis, and T.E. Sokoloski. 1989. SOIL-VEGETATION CORRELATIONS IN TRANSITION ZONES OF RHODE ISLAND RED MAPLE SWAMPS. (In Press.) US Fish and Wildlife Service, Washington, DC.

Baad, M.F. 1988. SOIL-VEGETATION CORRELATIONS WITHIN THE RIPARIAN ZONE OF BUTTE SINK IN THE SACRAMENTO VALLEY OF NORTHERN CALIFORNIA. US Fish and Wildlife Service, Washington, DC. Biol. Rpt. 88(25). 48 pp.

Christensen, N.L., R.B. Wilbur and J.S. McLean. 1988. SOIL-VEGETATION CORRELATIONS IN THE POCOSINS OF CROATAN NATIONAL FOREST. US Fish and Wildlife Service, Washington, DC. Biol. Rpt. 88(28). 97 pp.

Curtis, J. 1971. THE VEGETATION OF WISCONSIN. University of Wisconsin Press, Madison, WI. 657 pp.

Dick-Peddie, W.A., J.V. Hardesty, E. Muldavin, and B. Sallach. 1987. SOIL-VEGETATION CORRELATIONS ON THE RIPARIAN ZONES OF THE GILA AND SAN FRANCISCO RIVERS IN NEW MEXICO. US Fish and Wildlife Service, Washington, DC. Biol. Rpt. 87(9). 29 pp.

Eicher, A.L. 1988. SOIL-PLANT CORRELATIONS IN WETLANDS AND ADJACENT UPLANDS OF THE SAN FRANCISCO BAY ESTUARY, CALIFORNIA. US Fish and Wildlife Service, Washington, DC. Biol. Rpt. 88(21). 35 pp.

Erickson, M.E. and D.M. Leslie, Jr. 1987. SOIL-VEGETATION CORRELATIONS IN THE SANDHILLS AND RAINWATER BASIN WETLANDS OF NEBRASKA. US Fish and Wildlife Service, Washington, DC. Biol. Rpt. 87(11). 72 pp.

Erickson, N.E. and D.M. Leslie, Jr. 1989. SOIL-VEGETATION CORRELATIONS IN COASTAL MISSISSIPPI WETLANDS. (In Press.) US Fish and Wildlife Service, Washington, DC. 47 pp.

Hettinger, L.R., and A.J. Lanz. 1974. VEGETATION AND SOILS OF NORTHEASTERN ALASKA. Northern Engineering Services Company Limited, Arctic Gas. Biological Report Series, Vol. 21. 8 pp.

Hubbard, D.E., J.B. Millar, D.D. Malo, and K.F. Higgins. 1988. SOIL-VEGETATION CORRELATIONS IN PRAIRIE POTHOLES OF BEADLE AND DAUEL COUNTIES, SOUTH DAKOTA. US Fish and Wildlife Service, Washington, DC. Biol. Rpt. 88(22). 97 pp.

Nachlinger, J.L. 1988. SOIL-VEGETATION CORRELATIONS IN RIPARIAN AND EMERGENT WETLANDS, LYON COUNTY, NEVADA. US Fish and Wildlife Service, Washington, DC. Biol. Rpt. 88(17). 39 pp.

Palmisano, A.W., and R.H. Chabreck. 1972. THE RELATIONSHIP OF PLANT COMMUNITIES AND SOILS OF THE LOUISIANA COASTAL MARSHES. Proceedings of the Louisiana Assoc. of Agronomists.

Parker, W.B., S. Faulkner, B. Gambrell, and W.H. Patrick, Jr. 1984. SOIL WETNESS AND AERATION IN RELATION TO PLANT ADAPTATION FOR SELECTED HYDRIC SOILS IN THE MISSISSIPPI AND PEARL RIVER DELTAS. In: PROCEEDINGS OF WORKSHOP ON CHARACTERIZATION, CLASSIFICATION, AND UTILIZATION OF WETLAND SOILS (March 26-April 1, 1984). International Rice Research Institute, Los Banos, Laguna, Philippines.

VIII. COMMUNITY PROFILE AND ECOLOGICAL CHARACTERIZATION REPORTS

Bahr, L.M., and W.P. Lanier. 1981. THE ECOLOGY OF INTERTIDAL OYSTER REEFS OF THE SOUTH ATLANTIC COAST: A COMMUNITY PROFILE. US Fish and Wildlife Service, Washington, DC. Publ. No. FWS/OBS-81/15. 105 pp.

Brockway, D.G., C. Topik, M.A. Hemstrom, and W.H. Emmingham. 1983. PLANT ASSOCIATION AND MANAGEMENT GUIDE FOR THE PACIFIC SILVER FIR ZONE. USDA, Forest Service, Portland, OR. Publ. No. R6-ECOL-130a-1983.

Copeland, B.J., R.G. Hodson and S.R. Riggs. 1984. THE ECOLOGY OF THE PAMLICO RIVER, NORTH CAROLINA: AN ESTUARINE PROFILE. US Fish and Wildlife Service, Washington, DC. Publ. No. FWS/OBS-82/06. 83 pp.

Curtis, J.T. 1978. THE VEGETATION OF WISCONSIN. University of Wisconsin Press, Madison, WI. 657 pp.

Damman, A.W.H. and T.W. French. 1987. THE ECOLOGY OF PEAT BOGS IN THE GLACIATED NORTHEASTERN UNITED STATES: A COMMUNITY PROFILE. US Fish and Wildlife Service, Washington, DC. Biol. Rpt. 85(7.16). 100 pp.

Eyre, F.H. (editor). 1980. FOREST COVER TYPES OF THE UNITED STATES AND CANADA. Society of American Foresters, Washington, DC. 148 pp.

Fish and Wildlife Service. 1979. ECOLOGICAL CHARACTERIZATION OF THE SEA ISLAND COASTAL REGION OF SOUTH CAROLINA AND GEORGIA. 6 Vols. US Fish and Wildlife Service, Washington, DC. Publ. FWS/OBS-79/40, 79/41 & 79/42. Vol I-212 pp.; Vol II-321 pp.; Vol. III-620 pp.

Fish and Wildlife Service. 1980. AN ECOLOGICAL CHARACTERIZATION OF COASTAL MAINE. (Out of Print) US Fish and Wildlife Service, Washington, DC. Publ. No. FWS/OBS-80/29.

Fish and Wildlife Service. 1981. AN ECOLOGICAL CHARACTERIZATION OF THE CENTRAL AND NORTHERN CALIFORNIA COASTAL REGION. 5 Vols. US Fish and Wildlife Service, Washington, DC. Publ. Nos. FWS/OBS-80/45 - 80/49. Vol. I-209 pp.; Vol. 2-593 pp.; Vol III-1352 pp.; Vol. IV-1395 pp.; Vol. V-77 pp.

Fish and Wildlife Service. 1981. FISH AND WILDLIFE RESOURCES OF THE GREAT LAKES COASTAL WETLANDS WITHIN THE UNITED STATES. VOLUMES 1-6. US Fish and Wildlife Service, Washington, DC. Vol. 1-480 pp.; Vol 2-1351 pp.; Vol 3-530 pp.; Vol. 4-834 pp.; Vol 5-1676 pp.; Vol. 6-901 pp.

Fish and Wildlife Service. 1982. ALABAMA COASTAL REGION ECOLOGICAL CHARACTERIZATION: VOLUME 2. - A SYNTHESIS OF ENVIRONMENTAL DATA. US Fish and Wildlife Service, Washington, DC. Publ. No. FWS/OBS-82/42. 346 pp.

Glaser, P.H. 1987. THE ECOLOGY OF PATTERNED BOREAL PEATLANDS OF NORTHERN MINNESOTA: A COMMUNITY PROFILE. US Fish and Wildlife Service, Washington, DC. Biol. Rpt. 85 (7.14). 98 pp.

Gosselink, J.G. 1984. THE ECOLOGY OF DELTA MARSHES OF COASTAL LOUISIANA: A COMMUNITY PROFILE. US Fish and Wildlife Service, Washington, DC. Publ. No. FWS/OBS-84/09. 134 pp.

Halverson, N. M. 1986. MAJOR INDICATOR SHRUBS AND HERBS ON NATIONAL FORESTS OF WESTERN OREGON AND SOUTHWESTERN WASHINGTON. USDA, Forest Service, Portland, OR. Publ. No. R6-TM-229-1098.

Halverson, N.M., C. Topik, and R. Van Vickle. 1987. PLANT ASSOCIATION AND MANAGEMENT GUIDE FOR THE WESTERN HEMLOCK ZONE. USDA, Forest Service, Portland, OR. Publ. No. R6-ECOL-232A-1986.

Hansen, P.L., S.W. Chadde, and R.D. Pfister. 1987. RIPARIAN DOMINANCE TYPES OF MONTANA. Review Draft. Montana Riparian Association, University of Montana, Missoula, MT. 358 pp.
Heinecke, T.E. 1987. THE FLORA AND PLANT COMMUNITIES OF THE MIDDLE MISSISSIPPI RIVER VALLEY. Ph.D. Dissertation. Southern Illinois University, Carbondale, IL. 653 pp.

Herdendorf, C.E., C.N. Raphael, and E. Jawarski. 1986. THE ECOLOGY OF LAKE ST. CLAIR WET-LANDS: A COMMUNITY PROFILE. US Fish and Wildlife Service, Washington, DC. Biol. Rpt. 85 (7.7). 187 pp.

Herdendorf, C.E. 1987. THE ECOLOGY OF COASTAL MARSHES OF WESTERN LAKE ERIE: A COMMUNITY PROFILE. US Fish and Wildlife Service, Washington, DC. Biol. Rpt. 85(7.9). 240 pp.

Hobbie, J.E. 1984. THE ECOLOGY OF TUNDRA PONDS OF THE ARCTIC COASTAL PLAIN: A COMMUNITY PROFILE. US Fish and Wildlife Service, Washington, DC. Publ. No. FWS/OBS-83/25. 52 pp.

Holland, R.F. 1986. PRELIMINARY DESCRIPTIONS OF THE TERRESTRIAL NATURAL COM-MUNITIES OF CALIFORNIA. California Department of Fish and Game. Sacramento, CA. 156 pp.

Hopkins, W.E. 1979. PLANT ASSOCIATIONS OF THE FREMONT NATIONAL FOREST. USDA, Forest Service, Portland, OR. Publ. No. R6-ECOL-79-004. 106 pp.

Hopkins, W.E. 1979. PLANT ASSOCIATIONS OF SOUTH CHILOQUIN AND KLAMATH RANG-ER DISTRICTS - WINEMA NATIONAL FOREST. USDA, Forest Service, Portland, OR. Publ. No. R6-ECOL-79-005.

Hopkins, W.E., and B.L. Kovalchik. 1983. PLANT ASSOCIATIONS OF THE CROOKED RIVER NATIONAL GRASSLAND, OCHOCO NATIONAL FORESTS. USDA, Forest Service, Portland, OR. Publ. R6-ECOL-133-1983. 98 pp.

Josselyn, M. 1983. THE ECOLOGY OF SAN FRANCISCO BAY TIDAL MARSHES: A COMMUNI-TY PROFILE. US Fish and Wildlife Service, Washington, DC. Publ. No. FWS/OBS-83/23. 102 pp.

Kovalchik, B.L. 1987. RIPARIAN ZONE ASSOCIATIONS DESCHUTES, OCHOCO, FREMONT AND WINEMA NATIONAL FORESTS. USDA, Forest Service, Portland, OR. Publ. No. R6-ECOL-TP-274-87.

Kovalchik, B.E., W.E. Hopkins, and S.J. Brunsfeld. 1988. MAJOR INDICATOR SHRUBS AND HERBS IN RIPARIAN ZONES ON NATIONAL FORESTS OF CENTRAL OREGON. USDA, Forest Service, Portland, OR. Publ. No. R6-ECOL-TP-005-88.

Livingston, R.J. 1984. THE ECOLOGY OF APALACHICOLA BAY SYSTEM: AN ESTUARINE PRO-FILE. US Fish and Wildlife Service, Washington, DC. Publ. No. FWS/OBS-82/05. 148 pp.

Nixon, S.W. 1982. THE ECOLOGY OF NEW ENGLAND HIGH SALT MARSHES: A COMMUNITY PROFILE. US Fish and Wildlife Service, Washington, DC. Publ. No. FWS/OBS-81/55. 70 pp.

Odum, W.E., C.C. McIvor, and T.J. Smith III. 1982. THE ECOLOGY OF THE MANGROVES OF SOUTH FLORIDA: A COMMUNITY PROFILE. US Fish and Wildlife Service, Washington, DC. Publ. No. FWS/OBS-81.24.

Odum, W.E., T.J. Smith III, J.K. Hoover, and C.C. McIvor. 1984. THE ECOLOGY OF TIDAL FRESHWATER MARSHES OF THE UNITED STATES EAST COAST: A COMMUNITY PROFILE. US Fish and Wildlife Service, Washington, DC. Publ. No. FWS/OBS-83/17. 176 pp.

Omhart, R.D., B.W. Anderson, and W.C. Hunter. 1988. THE ECOLOGY OF THE LOWER COLORA-DO RIVER FROM DAVIS DAM TO THE MEXICO-UNITED STATES BOUNDARY: A COMMUNITY PROFILE. US Fish and Wildlife Service, Washington, DC. Biol. Rpt. 85(7.19). 296 pp.

Proctor, C.M., et al. 1980. ECOLOGICAL CHARACTERIZATION OF THE PACIFIC NORTHWEST COAST REGION. 5 Vols. US Fish and Wildlife Service, Washington, DC. Publ. No. FWS/OBS-79/11. Vol. 1-224 pp.; Vol. 2-574 pp.; Vol 3-327 pp.; Vol. 4-551 pp.; Vol 5-70 pp.

Schomer, N.S., and R.D. Drew. 1982. AN ECOLOGICAL CHARACTERIZATION OF THE LOWER EVERGLADES, FLORIDA BAY, AND THE FLORIDA KEYS. US Fish and Wildlife Service, Washington, DC. Publ. No. FWS/OBS-82/58.1. 263 pp.

Schomer, N.S., and R.D. Drew. 1982. AN ECOLOGICAL CHARACTERIZATION OF THE CALOO-SAHATCHEE RIVER/BIG CYPRESS WATERSHED. US Fish and Wildlife Service, Washington, DC. Publ. No. FWS/OBS-82/58.2. 225 pp.

Seliskar, D.M. and J.L. Gallagher. 1983. THE ECOLOGY OF TIDAL MARSHES OF THE PACIFIC NORTHWEST COAST: A COMMUNITY PROFILE. US Fish and Wildlife Service, Washington, DC. Publ. No. FWS/OBS-82/32. 65 pp.

Sharitz, R.R. and J.W. Gibbons. 1982. THE ECOLOGY OF SOUTHEASTERN SHRUB BOGS (POC-OSINS) AND CAROLINA BAYS: A COMMUNITY PROFILE. US Fish and Wildlife Service, Washington, DC. Publ. No. FWS/OBS-82/04. 93 pp.

Simenstad, C.A. 1983. THE ECOLOGY OF ESTUARINE CHANNELS OF THE PACIFIC NORTH-WEST COAST: A COMMUNITY PROFILE. US Fish and Wildlife Service, Washington, DC. Publ. No. FWS/OBS-83/05. 181 pp.

Stout, J.P. 1984. THE ECOLOGY OF IRREGULARLY FLOODED SALT MARSHES OF THE NORTHEASTERN GULF OF MEXICO: A COMMUNITY PROFILE. US Fish and Wildlife Service, Washington, DC. Biol. Rpt. 85(7.1). 98 pp.

Teal, J.M. 1985. THE ECOLOGY OF REGULARLY FLOODED SALT MARSHES OF NEW ENG-LAND. US Fish and Wildlife Service, Washington, DC. Publ. No. 85(7.4). 61 pp.

Volland, L.A. 1982. PLANT ASSOCIATIONS OF THE CENTRAL OREGON PUMICE ZONE. USDA, Forest Service, Portland, OR. Publ. No. R6-ECOL-104-1982.

Wharton, C.H., W.M. Kitchens, E.C. Pendleton, and T.W. Sipe. 1982. THE ECOLOGY OF BOTTOM-LAND HARDWOOD SWAMPS OF THE SOUTHEAST: A COMMUNITY PROFILE. US Fish and Wildlife Service, Washington, DC. Publ. No. FWS/OBS-81/37.

Whitlatch, R.B. 1982. THE ECOLOGY OF NEW ENGLAND TIDAL FLATS: A COMMUNITY PRO-FILE. US Fish and Wildlife Service, Washington, DC. Publ. No. FWS/OBS-81/01. 217 PP.

Wiedemann, A.M. 1984. THE ECOLOGY OF PACIFIC NORTHWEST COASTAL SAND DUNES: A COMMUNITY PROFILE. US Fish and Wildlife Service, Washington, DC. Publ. No. FWS/OBS-84/04. 1984.

Windell, J.T., B.E. Willard, D.J. Cooper, S.Q. Foster, C.F. Knud-hansen, L.P. Rink, and G.M. Kila-dis. 1986. AN ECOLOGICAL CHARACTERIZATION OF ROCKY MOUNTAIN MONTANE AND SUBALPINE WETLANDS. US Fish and Wildlife Service, Washington, DC. Biol. Rpt. 85(7.19). 298 pp.

Williams, C.K., and T.R. Lillybridge. 1983. FORESTED PLANT ASSOCIATIONS OF THE OKANO-GAN NATIONAL FOREST. USDA, Forest Service, Portland, OR. Publ. No. R6-ECOL-132-1983. 116 pp.

Williams, C.K., and T.R. Lillybridge. 1985. FORESTED PLANT ASSOCIATIONS OF THE COL-VILLE NATIONAL FOREST. (Draft). USDA, Forest Service. 96 pp.

Wolfe, S.H., and D.B. Menas. 1988. AN ECOLOGICAL CHARACTERIZATION OF THE FLORIDA PANHANDLE. US Fish and Wildlife Service, Washington, DC. Biol. Rpt. 99(12). 277 pp.

Zedler, J.B. 1982. THE ECOLOGY OF SOUTHERN CALIFORNIA COASTAL SALT MARSHES: A COMMUNITY PROFILE. US Fish and Wildlife Service, Washington, DC. Publ. No. FWS/OBS-81/54. 110 pp.

Zedler, P.H. 1987. THE ECOLOGY OF SOUTHERN CALIFORNIA VERNAL POOLS: A COMMUNITY PROFILE. US Fish and Wildlife Service, Washington, DC. Biol. Rpt. 85(7.11). 136 pp.

IX. OTHER WETLAND BOOKS OF INTEREST

Ash, A.N. 1983. NATURAL AND MODIFIED POCOSINS: LITERATURE SYNTHESIS AND MANAGEMENT OBJECTIVES. US Fish and Wildlife Service, Washington, DC. Publ. No. FWS/OBS-83/04. 156 pp.

Batten, A.R. 1980. A PROPOSED CLASSIFICATION FRAMEWORK FOR ALASKA WETLAND AND AQUATIC VEGETATION. Institute of Arctic Biology, University of Alaska, Fairbanks, AK. 135 pp.

Batten, A.R., and B.F. Murray. 1982. A LITERATURE SURVEY OF THE WETLAND VEGETATION OF ALASKA. Institute of Arctic Biology, University of Alaska, Fairbanks, AK. 222 pp.

Brabander, J.J., R.E. Masters, and R.M. Short. 1985. BOTTOMLAND HARDWOODS OF EASTERN OKLAHOMA. US Fish and Wildlife Service, Tulsa, OK and Oklahoma Department of Wildlife Conservation, Oklahoma City, OK. 83 pp + appendices.

Chabreck, R.H. 1972. VEGETATION, WATER AND SOIL CHARACTERISTICS OF THE LOUISIANA COASTAL REGION. Louisiana Agricultural Experiment Station, Baton Rouge, LA. Bull. 664. 72 p.

Clark, J.R. and J. Benforado (editors). 1981. WETLANDS OF BOTTOMLAND HARDWOOD FORESTS; PROCEEDINGS OF A WORKSHOP ON BOTTOMLAND HARDWOOD FOREST WETLANDS OF THE SOUTHEASTERN UNITED STATES. Elsevier Scientific Publishing Company, NY.

Cowardin, L.M., V. Carter, F.C. Golet, and E.T. LaRoe. 1979. CLASSIFICATION OF WETLANDS AND DEEPWATER HABITATS OF THE UNITED STATES. US Fish and Wildlife Service, Office of Biological Services, Washington, DC. Publ. No. FWS/OBS-79/31. 107 pp.

Environmental Laboratory. 1987. CORPS OF ENGINEERS WETLANDS DELINEATION MANUAL. US Army Engineer Waterways Experiment Station, Vicksburg, MS. Tech. Rpt. Y-87-1. 100 pp. plus appendices.

Eyre, F.H. (editor) 1980. FOREST COVER TYPES OF THE UNITED STATES AND CANADA. Society of American Foresters, Washington, DC. 148 pp.

Good, R.E., D.F. Whigham, and R.L. Simpson (editors). 1978. FRESHWATER WETLANDS. Academic Press, New York, NY.

Groman, H.A., T.R. Henderson, E.J. Meyers, D.M. Burke, and J.A. Kusler (editors). 1985. WETLANDS OF THE CHESAPEAKE. Environmental Law Institute, Washington, DC.

Hall, L.C. 1968. BIBLIOGRAPHY OF FRESHWATER WETLANDS ECOLOGY AND MANAGE-MENT. Department of Natural Resources, Madison, WI. Res. Rpt. No. 33.

Hook, D.D. 1978. PLANT LIFE IN ANAEROBIC ENVIRONMENTS. Ann Arbor Science Publishers, Inc., Ann Arbor, MI. 564 pp.

Hubbard, D.E. 1988. GLACIATED PRAIRIE WETLAND FUNCTIONS AND VALUES: A SYNTHE-SIS OF THE LITERATURE. US Fish and Wildlife Service, Washington, DC. Biol. Rpt. 88(43). 50 pp.

Kozlowski, T.T. (editor) 1984. FLOODING AND PLANT GROWTH. Academic Press, Inc., Orlando, FL. 356 pp.

Laderman, A.D. (editor) 1987. ATLANTIC WHITE CEDAR WETLANDS. Westview Press, Inc., Boulder, CO.

Lindstrom, L.E. 1968. THE AQUATIC AND MARSH PLANTS OF THE GREAT PLAINS OF CEN-TRAL NORTH AMERICA. Ph.D. Thesis, Kansas State University, Manhattan, KS. 247 pp.

Markovits, P.S. (editor). 1981. PROCEEDINGS - U.S. FISH AND WILDLIFE SERVICE WORK-SHOP ON COASTAL ECOSYSTEMS OF THE SOUTHEASTERN UNITED STATES. US Fish and Wildlife Service, Washington, DC. Publ. No. FWS/OBS-80/59. 257 pp.

McCormick, J. 1970. THE PINE BARRENS: A PRELIMINARY ECOLOGICAL INVENTORY. New Jersey State Museum, Trenton, NJ. Research Report No. 2. 100 pp.

McDonald, C.B. 1983. POCOSINS: A CHANGING WETLAND RESOURCE. US Fish and Wildlife Service, Washington, DC. Publ. No. FWS/OBS-83/32. 22 pp.

Mitsch, W.J., et al. 1983. ATLAS OF WETLANDS IN THE PRINCIPAL COAL SURFACE MINING REGION OF WESTERN KENTUCKY. US Fish and Wildlife Service, Washington, DC. Publ. No. FWS/OBS-82/72. 134 pp.

Mitsch, W.J. and J.G. Gosselink. 1986. WETLANDS. Van Nostrand Reinhold Co., Inc., New York, NY.

Niering, W.A. 1984. WETLANDS. Alfred A. Knopf, Inc., New York, NY.

Novitzki, R.P. 1979. AN INTRODUCTION TO WISCONSIN WETLANDS: PLANTS, HYDROLOGY, AND SOILS. US Geological Survey in cooperation with the University of Wisconsin. 19 pp.

Office of Technology Assessment. 1984. WETLANDS: THEIR USE AND REGULATION. US Congress, Washington, DC.

Penfound, W.T. 1952. SOUTHERN SWAMPS AND MARSHES. *Bot. Rev.* 18(6): 413-446.

Sipple, W.S. 1987. WETLAND IDENTIFICATION AND DELINEATION MANUAL. VOLUME I. RA-TIONALE, WETLAND PARAMETERS, AND OVERVIEW OF JURISDICTIONAL APPROACH. U.S. Environmental Protection Agency, Office of Wetlands Protection, Washington, DC. 28 pp. plus appendices.

Sipple, W.S. 1987. WETLAND IDENTIFICATION AND DELINEATION MANUAL. VOLUME II. FIELD METHODOLOGY. U.S. Environmental Protection Agency, Office of Wetlands Protection, Washington, DC. 29 pp. plus appendices.

Tiner, R.W. Jr. 1984. WETLANDS OF THE UNITED STATES: CURRENT STATUS AND RECENT TRENDS. US Fish and Wildlife Service, Washington, DC.

Tiner, R.W., Jr. 1985. WETLANDS OF DELAWARE. U.S. Fish and Wildlife Service, Newton Corner, MA and Delaware Department of Natural Resources and Environmental Control, Dover, DE. Cooperative Publication. 77 pp.

Tiner, R.W. Jr. 1985. WETLANDS OF NEW JERSEY. U.S. Fish and Wildlife Service, Newton Corner, MA. 117 pp.

Wolf, R.B., L.C.Lee, and R.R. Sharitz. 1986. WETLAND CREATION AND RESTORATION IN THE UNITED STATES FROM 1970 TO 1985: AN ANNOTATED BIBLIOGRAPHY. SPECIAL ISSUE. Wetlands 6(1):1-87.

Appendix B
Examples of Data Sheets

DATA FORM
ROUTINE ONSITE DETERMINATION METHOD[1]

Field Investigator(s): _____ Date: _____

Project/Site:_____ State: _____ County: _____

Applicant/Owner: _____ Plant Community #/Name: _____

Note: If a more detailed site description is necessary, use the back of data form or a field notebook.

- -

Do normal environmental conditions exist at the plant community?
Yes _____ No _____ (If no, explain on back)
Has the vegetation, soils, and/or hydrology been significantly disturbed?
Yes _____ No _____ (If yes, explain on back)

- -

VEGETATION

Dominant Plant Species	Indicator Status	Stratum	Dominant Plant Species	Indicator Status	Stratum
1. _____	___	___	11. _____	___	___
2. _____	___	___	12. _____	___	___
3. _____	___	___	13. _____	___	___
4. _____	___	___	14. _____	___	___
5. _____	___	___	15. _____	___	___
6. _____	___	___	16. _____	___	___
7. _____	___	___	17. _____	___	___
8. _____	___	___	18. _____	___	___
9. _____	___	___	19. _____	___	___
10. _____	___	___	20. _____	___	___

Percent of dominant species that are OBL, FACW, and/or FAC _____
Is the hydrophytic vegetation criterion met? Yes _____ No _____
Rationale: _____

SOILS

Series/phase: _____ Subgroup:[2] _____

Is the soil on the hydric soils list? Yes _____ No _____ Undetermined _____

Is the soil a Histosol? Yes _____ No _____ Histic epipedon present? Yes _____ No _____

Is the soil: Mottled? Yes _____ No _____ Gleyed? Yes _____ No _____

Matrix Color: _____ Mottle Colors: _____

Other hydric soil indicators: _____

Is the hydric soil criterion met? Yes _____ No _____

Rationale: _____

HYDROLOGY

Is the ground surface inundated? Yes _____ No _____ Surface water depth: _____

Is the soil saturated? Yes _____ No _____

Depth to free-standing water in pit/soil probe hole: _____

List other field evidence of surface inundation or soil saturation.

Is the wetland hydrology criterion met? Yes _____ No _____

Rationale: _____

JURISDICTIONAL DETERMINATION AND RATIONALE

Is the plant community a wetland? Yes _____ No _____
Rationale for jurisdictional decision: _____

[1] This data form can be used for the Hydric Soil Assessment Procedure and the Plant Community Assessment Procedure.

[2] Classification according to "Soil Taxonomy."

DATA FORM
INTERMEDIATE-LEVEL ONSITE DETERMINATION METHOD
QUADRAT TRANSECT SAMPLING PROCEDURE
(Vegetation Data)

Field Investigator(s): _____

Project/Site: _____ Date: _____

Applicant/Owner: _____ State: _____ County: _____

Transect # _____ Plot # _____

Note: If a more detailed site description is necessary, use the back of data form or a field notebook.

- -

DOMINANT PLANT SPECIES

Herbs (Bryophytes)	Indicator Status	Saplings	Indicator Status
1.		1.	
2.		2.	
3.		3.	
4.		4.	
5.		5.	
6.		6.	
7.		7.	
8.		8.	
9.		9.	
10.		10.	
11.		11.	
12.		12.	
13.		13.	

Shrubs		Trees	
1.		1.	
2.		2.	
3.		3.	
4.		4.	
5.		5.	
6.		6.	
7.		7.	
8.		8.	
9.		9.	
10.		10.	
11.		11.	
12.		12.	
13.		13.	

Woody Vines	
1.	
2.	
3.	
4.	
5.	
6.	
7.	
8.	
9.	
10.	
11.	
12.	
13.	

Percent of dominant species that are OBL, FACW, and/or FAC _____

DATA FORM
INTERMEDIATE-LEVEL ONSITE DETERMINATION METHOD
VEGETATION UNIT SAMPLING PROCEDURE
(Herbs and Bryophytes)

Field Investigator(s): _____ Date: _____

Project/Site:_____ State:_____ County: _____

Applicant/Owner: _____Vegetation Unit #/Name:_____

Note: If a more detailed site description is necessary, use the back of data form or a field notebook.

- -

Species	Indicator Status	Percent Areal Cover	Cover[1] Class	Midpoint[1] of Cover Class	Rank[2]
1.					
2.					
3.					
4.					
5.					
6.					
7.					
8.					
9.					
10.					
11.					
12.					
13.					
14.					
15.					
16.					
17.					
18.					
19.					
20.					
21.					
22.					
23.					
24.					
25.					
26.					
27.					
28.					
29.					
30.					
31.					
32.					
33.					
34.					
35.					
36.					

Sum of Midpoints _____

Dominance Threshold Number Equals 50% x Sum of Midpoints _____

- -

[1] Cover classes (midpoints): T<1% (none); 1 = 1-5% (3.0); 2 = 6-15% (10.5); 3 = 16-25% (20.5); 4 = 26-50% (38.0); 5 = 51-75% (63.0); 6 = 76-95% (85.5); 7 = 96-100% (98.0).

[2] To determine the dominants, first rank the species by their midpoints. Then cumulatively sum the midpoints of the ranked species until 50% of the total for all species midpoints is immediately exceeded. All species contributing to that cumulative total (the dominance threshold number) *plus* any additional species having 20% of the total midpoint value should be considered dominants and marked with an asterisk.

DATA FORM
INTERMEDIATE-LEVEL ONSITE DETERMINATION METHOD
VEGETATION UNIT SAMPLING PROCEDURE
(Shrubs, Woody Vines and Saplings)

Field Investigator(s): _____ Date: _____

Project/Site:_____ State: _____ County: _____

Applicant/Owner: _____Vegetation Unit #/Name:_____

Note: If a more detailed site description is necessary, use the back of data form or a field notebook.

- -

Shrub Species	Indicator Status	Percent Areal Cover	Cover[1] Class	Midpoint[1] of Cover Class	Rank[2]
1.					
2.					
3.					
4.					
5.					
6.					
7.					
8.					
9.					
10.					

Sum of Midpoints _____

Dominance Threshold Number Equals 50% x Sum of Midpoints _____

- -

Woody Vine Species	Indicator Status	Percent Areal Cover	Cover[1] Class	Midpoint[1] of Cover Class	Rank[2]
1.					
2.					
3.					
4.					
5.					

Sum of Midpoints _____

Dominance Threshold Number Equals 50% x Sum of Midpoints _____

- -

Sapling Species	Indicator Status	Percent Areal Cover	Cover[1] Class	Midpoint[1] of Cover Class	Rank[2]
1.					
2.					
3.					
4.					
5.					
6.					
7.					
8.					
9.					

Sum of Midpoints _____

Dominance Threshold Number Equals 50% x Sum of Midpoints _____

- -

[1] Cover classes (midpoints): T<1% (none); 1 = 1-5% (3.0); 2 = 6-15% (10.5); 3 = 16-25% (20.5); 4 = 26-50% (38.0); 5 = 51-75% (63.0); 6 = 76-95% (85.5); 7 = 96-100% (98.0).

[2] To determine the dominants, first rank the species by their midpoints. Then cumulatively sum the midpoints of the ranked species until 50% of the total for all species midpoints is immediately exceeded. All species contributing to that cumulative total (the dominance threshold number) *plus* any additional species having 20% of the total midpoint value should be considered dominants and marked with an asterisk.

DATA FORM
INTERMEDIATE-LEVEL ONSITE DETERMINATION METHOD
VEGETATION UNIT SAMPLING PROCEDURE
(Trees)

Field Investigator(s): _____ Date: _____

Project/Site:_____ State: _____ County: _____

Applicant/Owner: _____Vegetation Unit #/Name:_____

Note: If a more detailed site description is necessary, use the back of data form or a field notebook.

- -

Tree Species (Percent Cover Option)	Indicator Status	Percent Areal Cover	Cover[1] Class	Midpoint[1] of Cover Class	Rank[2]
1.					
2.					
3.					
4.					
5.					
6.					
7.					

Sum of Midpoints _____

Dominance Threshold Number Equals 50% x Sum of Midpoints _____

- -

Tree Species (Basal Area Option)	Indicator Status	Tally 1 2 3 4 5 6 7 8	Total Trees	Basal[3] Area	Rank[2]
1.					
2.					
3.					
4.					
5.					
6.					
7.					
8.					
9.					
10.					

Basal Area Factor (e.g., Prism Used) _____

Total Basal Area of All Species Combined _____

Dominance Threshold Number Equals 50% of Total Basal Area _____

- -

[1] Cover classes (midpoints): T<1% (none); 1 = 1-5% (3.0); 2 = 6-15% (10.5); 3 = 16-25% (20.5); 4 = 26-50% (38.0); 5 = 51-75% (63.0); 6 = 76-95% (85.5); 7 = 96-100% (98.0).

[2] To determine the dominants, first rank the species by their midpoints (or basal area). Then cumulatively sum the midpoints (basal area) of the ranked species until 50% of the total for all species midpoints (or basal area) is immediately exceeded. All species contributing to that cumulative total (the dominance threshold number) *plus* any additional species having 20% of the total midpoint, or basal area, value should be considered dominants and marked with an asterisk.

[3] The basal area for a species (on a per acre basis) is determined by dividing the total number of individual trees tallied for all tally areas by the number of tallies and multiplying by the basal area factor.

DATA FORM [1]
INTERMEDIATE-LEVEL ONSITE DETERMINATION METHOD OR
COMPREHENSIVE ONSITE DETERMINATION METHOD
(Soils and Hydrology)

Field Investigator(s): _____ Date: _____

Project/Site: _____ State: _____ County: _____

Applicant/Owner: _____

Intermediate-level Onsite Determination Method _____

Comprehensive Onsite Determination Method _____

Transect # _____ Plot # _____

Vegetation Unit #/Name: _____ Sample # Within Veg. Unit: _____

Note: If a more detailed site description is necessary, use the back of data form or a field notebook.

- -

SOILS

Series/phase: _____ Subgroup:[2] _____

Is the soil on the hydric soils list?   Yes _____   No _____   Undetermined _____

Is the soil a Histosol? Yes _____   No _____ Histic epipedon present? Yes _____ No _____

Is the soil: Mottled?   Yes _____   No _____ Gleyed? Yes _____   No _____

Matrix Color: _____ Mottle Colors: _____

Other hydric soil indicators: _____

Comments: _____
_____

- -

HYDROLOGY

Is the ground surface inundated? Yes _____   No _____   Surface water depth: _____

Is the soil saturated? Yes _____   No _____

Depth to free-standing water in pit/soil probe hole: _____

Mark other field indicators of surface inundation or soil saturation below:

_____ Oxidized root zones   _____ Water-stained leaves

_____ Water marks   _____ Surface scoured areas

_____ Drift lines   _____ Wetland drainage patterns

_____ Water-borne sediment deposits   _____ Morphological plant adaptations

Additional hydrologic indicators: _____
_____
_____

Comments: _____
_____
_____
_____
_____
_____

[1] This data form can be used for both the Vegetation Unit Sampling Procedure and the Quadrat Transect Sampling Procedure of the Intermediate-Level Onsite Determination Method, or the Quadrat Sampling Procedure of the Comprehensive Onsite Determination Method. Indicate which method is used.

[2] Classification according to "Soil Taxonomy."

DATA FORM [1]
INTERMEDIATE-LEVEL ONSITE DETERMINATION METHOD OR
COMPREHENSIVE ONSITE DETERMINATION METHOD
(Summary Sheet)

Field Investigator(s): _____ Date: _____

Project/Site:_____ State: _____ County: _____

Applicant/Owner:_____

Intermediate-level Onsite Determination Method _____

Comprehensive Onsite Determination Method _____

Transect # _____ Plot # _____ Vegetation Unit #/Name: _____

Note: If a more detailed site description is necessary, use the back of data form or a field notebook.

- -

Do normal environmental conditions exist at the plant community?

Yes _____ No _____ (If no, explain on back)

Has the vegetation, soils, and/or hydrology been significantly disturbed?

Yes _____ No _____ (If yes, explain on back)

Dominant Plant Species	Indicator Status	Stratum	Dominant Plant Species	Indicator Status	Stratum
1.			14.		
2.			15.		
3.			16.		
4.			17.		
5.			18.		
6.			19.		
7.			20.		
8.			21.		
9.			22.		
10.			23.		
11.			24.		
12.			25.		
13.			26.		

- -

Percent of dominant species that are OBL, FACW and/or FAC _____

Is the hydrophytic vegetation criterion met? Yes _____ No _____

Is the hydric soil criterion met? Yes _____ No _____

Is the wetland hydrology criterion met? Yes _____ No _____

Is the vegetation unit or plot wetland? Yes _____ No _____

Rationale for jurisdictional decision: _____

_____

_____

[1] This data form can be used for either the Intermediate-level Onsite Determination Method or the Comprehensive Onsite Determination Method. Indicate which method is used.

DATA FORM
COMPREHENSIVE ONSITE DETERMINATION METHOD
QUADRAT SAMPLING PROCEDURE [1]
(Herbs and Bryophytes)

Field Investigator(s): _____ Date: _____

Project/Site: _____ State: _____ County: _____

Applicant/Owner: _____

Transect # _____ Plot # _____ Vegetation Unit #/Name: _____

Note: If a more detailed site description is necessary, use the back of data form or a field notebook.

Species	Indicator Status	Quadrat Percent Areal Cover								$\bar{X}$	Rank[4]
		Q1	Q2	Q3	Q4	Q5	Q6	Q7	Q8		
1.											
2.											
3.											
4.											
5.											
6.											
7.											
8.											
9.											
10.											
11.											
12.											
13.											
14.											
15.											
16.											

Total Cover ____ [2]

Dominance Threshold Number Equals 50% x Total Cover ____ [2]

Total of Averages ($\bar{X}$'s) ____ [3]

Dominance Threshold Number Equals 50% x Total of Averages ($\bar{X}$'s) ____ [3]

---

[1] This data form can be used for both the Plant Community Transect Sampling Approach and the Fixed Interval Transect Sampling Approach.

[2] These entries are only applicable to the Fixed Interval Transect Sampling Approach which uses only one quadrat per sampling point along a transect.

[3] These entries are only applicable to the Plant Community Transect Sampling Approach which uses multiple quadrats per sampling point along a transect.

[4] To determine the dominants, first rank the species by their cover (or mean cover). Then cumulatively sum the cover (mean cover) of the ranked species until 50% of the total for all species cover (mean cover) is immediately exceeded. All species contributing to that cumulative total (the dominance threshold number) *plus* additional species having 20% of the total cover (mean cover) value should be considered dominants and marked with an asterisk.

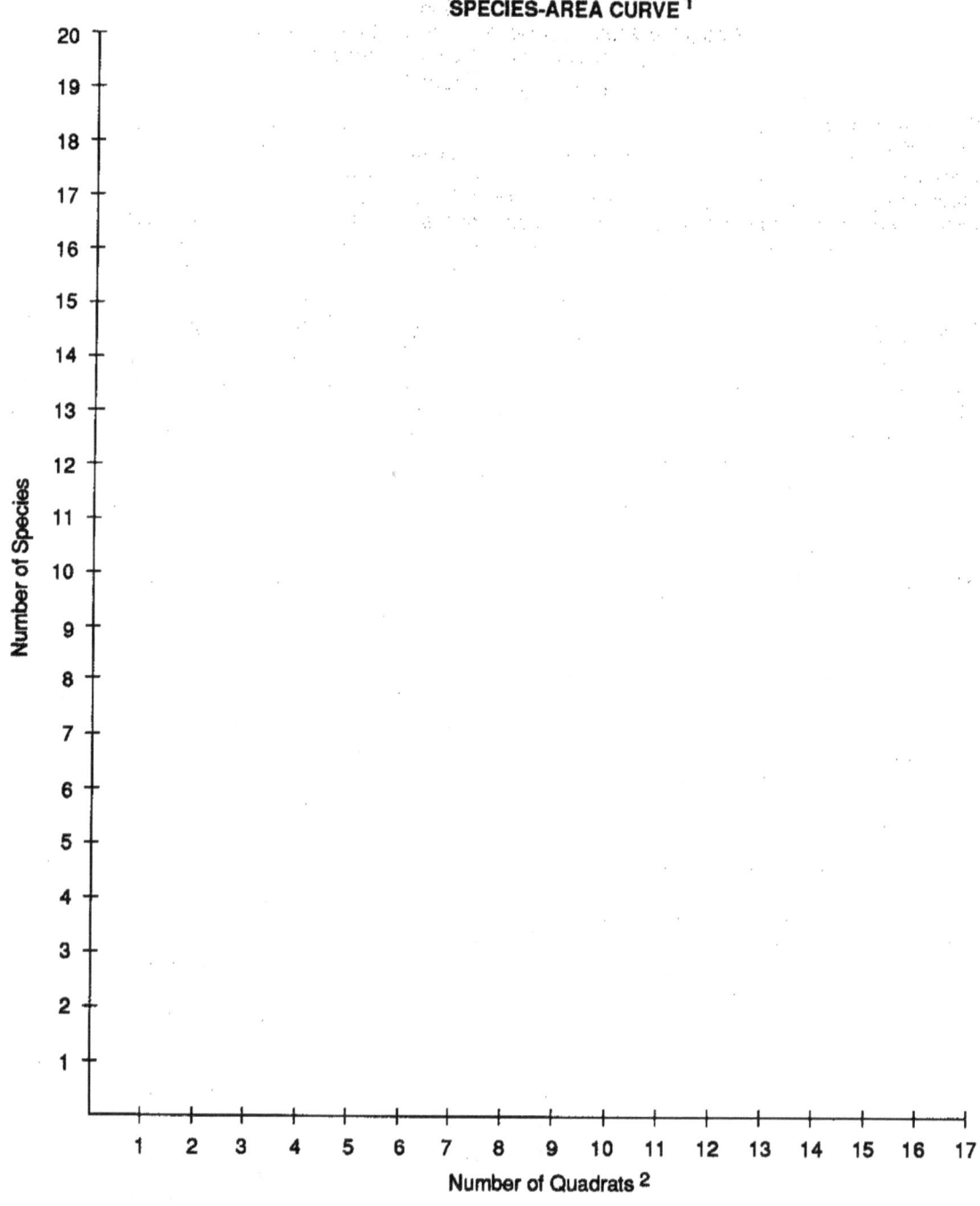

SPECIES-AREA CURVE [1]

Number of Species (y-axis: 1 to 20)

Number of Quadrats [2] (x-axis: 1 to 17)

[1] Plot the cumulative number of species against the quadrats (e.g., if quadrat #1 has 3 species and quadrat #2 has any, all, or none of those species but has 2 new species, then 5 cumulative species should be plotted against quadrat #2). The number of quadrats sufficient to adequately survey the understory will corresdpond to the point on the curve where it first levels off and remains essentially level.

[2] Specify size of sample quadrat: _____

DATA FORM
COMPREHENSIVE ONSITE DETERMINATION METHOD
QUADRAT SAMPLING PROCEDURE
(Shrubs and Woody Vines)

Field Investigator(s): _____ Date: _____

Project/Site: _____ State: _____ County: _____

Applicant/Owner: _____

Transect # _____ Plot # _____ Vegetation Unit #/Name: _____

Note: If a more detailed site description is necessary, use the back of data form or a field notebook.

Shrub Species	Indicator Status	Percent Areal Cover	Cover[1] Class	Midpoint[1] of Cover Class	Rank[2]
1.					
2.					
3.					
4.					
5.					
6.					
7.					
8.					
9.					
10.					
11.					
12.					
13.					
14.					

Sum of Midpoints _____

Dominance Threshold Number Equals 50% x Sum of Midpoints _____

Woody Vine Species	Indicator Status	Percent Areal Cover	Cover[1] Class	Midpoint[1] of Cover Class	Rank[2]
1.					
2.					
3.					
4.					
5.					
6.					
7.					
8.					
9.					
10.					
11.					
12.					
13.					
14.					

Sum of Midpoints _____

Dominance Threshold Number Equals 50% x Sum of Midpoints _____

[1] Cover classes (midpoints): T<1% (none); 1 = 1-5% (3.0); 2 = 6-15% (10.5); 3 = 16-25% (20.5); 4 = 26-50% (38.0); 5 = 51-75% (63.0); 6 = 76-95% (85.5); 7 = 96-100% (98.0).

[2] To determine the dominants, first rank the species by their midpoints. Then cumulatively sum the midpoints of the ranked species until 50% of the total for all species midpoints is immediately exceeded. All species contributing to that cumulative total (the dominance threshold number) *plus* any additional species having 20% of the total midpoint value should be considered dominants and marked with an asterisk.

DATA FORM
COMPREHENSIVE ONSITE DETERMINATION METHOD
QUADRAT SAMPLING PROCEDURE
(Saplings & Trees)

Field Investigator(s): _____ Date: _____

Project/Site: _____ State: _____ County: _____

Applicant/Owner: _____

Transect # _____ Plot # _____ Vegetation Unit #/Name: _____

Note: If a more detailed site description is necessary, use the back of data form or a field notebook.

Sapling Species	Indicator Status	Percent Areal Cover	Cover[1] Class	Midpoint[1] of Cover Class	Rank[2]
1.					
2.					
3.					
4.					
5.					
6.					
7.					
8.					
9.					
10.					

Sum of Midpoints _____

Dominance Threshold Number Equals 50% x Sum of Midpoints _____

Individual Tree Species	Indicator Status	DBH (inches)	Basal Area (BA) Per Tree (sq ft)	BA Per Species (sq ft)	Rank[2]
1.					
2.					
3.					
4.					
5.					
6.					
7.					
8.					
9.					
10.					
11.					
12.					
13.					
14.					
15.					
16.					

Total Basal Area of All Species Combined _____

Dominance Threshold Number Equals 50% x Total Basal Area _____

[1] Cover classes (midpoints): T<1% (none); 1 = 1-5% (3.0); 2 = 6-15% (10.5); 3 = 16-25% (20.5); 4 = 26-50% (38.0); 5 = 51-75% (63.0); 6 = 76-95% (85.5); 7 = 96-100% (98.0).

[2] To determine the dominants, first rank the species by their midpoints. Then cumulatively sum the midpoints of the ranked species until 50% of the total for all species midpoints is immediately exceeded. All species contributing to that cumulative total (the dominance threshold number) *plus* any additional species having 20% of the total midpoint value should be considered dominants and marked with an asterisk.

PREVALENCE INDEX WORKSHEET

LOCATION _____ DATE _____ EVALUATOR _____

HYDRIC UNIT NAME _____ TRANSECT NO. _____

Frequency of Occurrence of Identified Plants
with Known Indicator Status

Plant Species	Frequency of Occurrence Total for Each Species	F_o Obligate	F_{fw} Facult. Wet.	F_f Facult.	F_{fu} Facult. Upland	F_u Upland
_____	_____	____	_____	_____	_____	_____
_____	_____	____	_____	_____	_____	_____
_____	_____	____	_____	_____	_____	_____
_____	_____	____	_____	_____	_____	_____
_____	_____	____	_____	_____	_____	_____
_____	_____	____	_____	_____	_____	_____
_____	_____	____	_____	_____	_____	_____
_____	_____	____	_____	_____	_____	_____
_____	_____	____	_____	_____	_____	_____
_____	_____	____	_____	_____	_____	_____
_____	_____	____	_____	_____	_____	_____
_____	_____	____	_____	_____	_____	_____
_____	_____	____	_____	_____	_____	_____
_____	_____	____	_____	_____	_____	_____
_____	_____	____	_____	_____	_____	_____
_____	_____	____	_____	_____	_____	_____
_____	_____	____	_____	_____	_____	_____

Total occurrence for all plant species _____ _____ _____ _____ _____ _____

Total occurrences ID'd with known indicator status _____ _____ _____ _____ _____ _____

E.I. value 1 2 3 4 5

$$\frac{\text{Total occurrences identified with known indicator status}}{\text{Total occurrence for all plant species}} = \% \text{ valid occurrences}$$

$$PI_i = \frac{(1F_o) + (2F_{fw}) + (3F_f) + (4F_{fu}) + (5F_u)}{(F_o + F_{fw} + F_f + F_{fu} + F_u)}$$

Appendix C
Sample Calculation for Herb Stratum Dominants

DATA FORM
COMPREHENSIVE ONSITE DETERMINATION METHOD
QUADRAT SAMPLING PROCEDURE[1]
(Herbs and Bryophytes)

Field Investigator(s): _Bob Barber and Bill Sipple_ Date: _7/29/87_

Project/Site: _Weise Slough_ State: _Iowa_ County: _Muscatine_

Applicant/Owner: _State of Iowa_

Transect # _1_ Plot # _2_ Vegetation Unit #/Name: _#1/Marsh_

Note: If a more detailed site description is necessary, use the back of data form or a field notebook.

Species	Indicator Status	Q1	Q2	Q3	Q4	Q5	Q6	Q7	Q8	X̄	Rank[4]
*1. Leersia oryzoides	OBL	95	99	99	100	<1	30	20	20	57.9	1
2. Echinochloa muricata			2	5	5	15		2	2	3.88	4
3. Lemna sp.		70	20		5					11.88	2
4. UI Seedling (herb)		<1		<1	<1	<1	15	<1		1.88	6
5. Bidens sp.			1	2		1	10	10	2	3.25	5
6. Sagittaria latifolia			<1	<1						—	7
7. Rumex verticillatus						80				10	3
8.											
9.											
10.											
11.											
12.											
13.											
14.											
15.											
16.											

Total Cover __2

Dominance Threshold Number Equals 50% x Total Cover __2

Total of Averages (X̄'s) _88.8_ [3]

Dominance Threshold Number Equals 50% x Total of Averages (X̄'s) _44.4_ [3]

- -

[1] This data form can be used for both the Plant Community Transect Sampling Approach and the Fixed Interval Transect Sampling Approach.

[2] These entries are only applicable to the Fixed Interval Transect Sampling Approach which uses only one quadrat per sampling point along a transect.

[3] These entries are only applicable to the Plant Community Transect Sampling Approach which uses multiple quadrats per sampling point along a transect.

[4] To determine the dominants, first rank the species by their cover (or mean cover). Then cumulatively sum the cover (mean cover) of the ranked species until 50% of the total for all species cover (mean cover) is immediately exceeded. All species contributing to that cumulative total (the dominance threshold number) plus additional species having 20% of the total cover (mean cover) value should be considered dominants and marked with an asterisk.

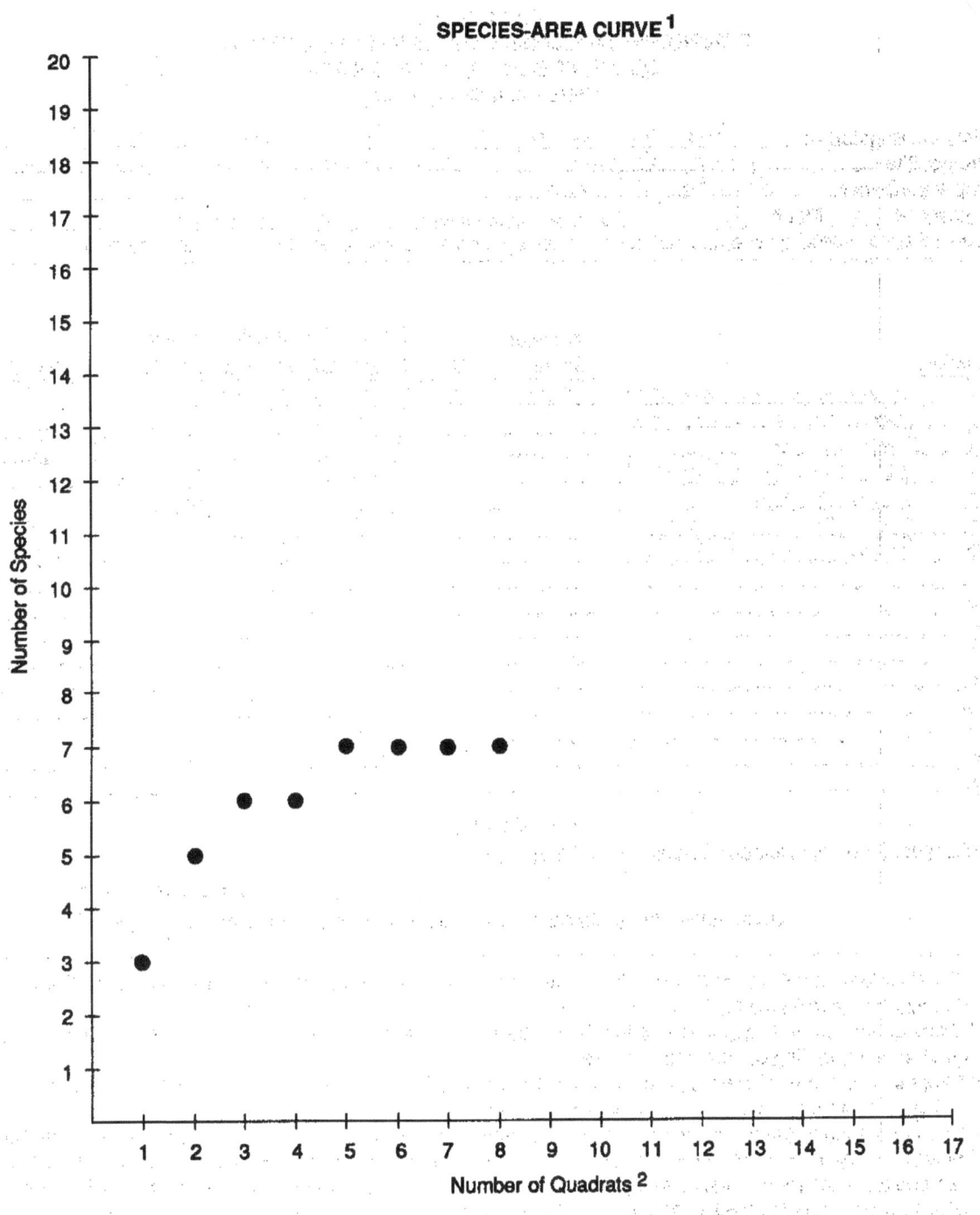

SPECIES-AREA CURVE [1]

Number of Species (y-axis, 1–20)

Number of Quadrats [2] (x-axis, 1–17)

[1] Plot the cumulative number of species against the quadrats (e.g., if quadrat #1 has 3 species and quadrat #2 has any, all, or none of those species but has 2 new species, then 5 cumulative species should be plotted against quadrat #2). The number of quadrats sufficient to adequately survey the understory will corresdpond to the point on the curve where it first levels off and remains essentially level.

[2] Specify size of sample quadrat: _____ *0.1 m²* _____

Appendix D
Sample Problem for Application of Point Intercept Sampling Method

Sample problem for application of point sampling method. Example follows this sample worksheet.

PREVALENCE INDEX WORKSHEET

LOCATION _Montgomery Co., MD_ _Farm 2164, Tract 742_ DATE _8/4/88_ EVALUATOR _Anne Lynn_

HYDRIC UNIT NAME _Bibb_ TRANSECT NO. _1_

Frequency of Occurrence of Identified Plants
with Known Indicator Status

Plant Species	Frequency of Occurrence Total for Each Species	F_o Obligate	F_{fw} Facult. Wet.	F_f Facult.	F_{fu} Facult. Upland	F_u Upland
Lirodendron Tulipifera	13				13	
Platanus occidentalis	20		20			
Acer rubrum	8			8		
Hedera holix	1					
Alnus serrulata	2	2				
Podophyllum peltatum	3					
Liquidambar styraciflua	2			2		
Galium asperllum	2	2				
Lindera benzoin	3		3			
Lonicera japonica	5			5		
Toxidendron radicans	5			5		
Viburnum recognitum	2		2			
Arisaema Triphyllum	4		4			
Carpinus caroliniana	2			2		
Ilex opaca	12				12	
Thelypteris noveboracensis	2			2		
Total occurrence for all plant species	86					
Total occurrences ID'd with known indicator status	82	4	29	24	25	
E.I. value		1	2	3	4	5

$$\frac{\text{Total occurrences identified with known indicator status}}{\text{Total occurrence for all plant species}} = \% \text{ valid occurrences} = 100 \times \frac{82}{86} \approx 95\%$$

$$PI_i = \frac{(1F_o) + (2F_{fw}) + (3F_f) + (4F_{fu}) + (5F_u)}{(F_o + F_{fw} + F_f + F_{fu} + F_u)}$$

COMPUTATIONS

1. Computation of prevalence index (PI) for transect #1:

$$PI_i = \frac{(1F_o) + (2F_{fw}) + (3F_f) + (4F_{fu}) + (5F_u)}{(F_o + F_{fw} + F_f + F_{fu} + F_u)}$$

$$PI_1 = \frac{(1 \times 4) + (2 \times 29) + (3 \times 24) + (4 \times 25)}{4 + 29 + 24 + 25} = \frac{234}{82} = 2.85$$

where:

PI_i = Prevalence index for transect i

F_o = Frequence of occurrence of obligate wetland species

F_{fw} = Frequency of occurrence of facultative wetland species

F_f = Frequency of occurrence of facultative species

F_{fu} = Frequency of occurrence of facultative upland species

F_u = Frequency of occurrence of upland species

2. Computation of mean prevalence index (PI_M) for three transects:

$$PI_M = \frac{PI_T}{N}$$

where:

PI_M = Mean prevalence index for transects

PI_T = Sum of prevalence index values for all transects

N = Total number of transects

For example: PI for Transect 1 = 2.85
                      PI for Transect 2 = 3.16
                      PI for Transect 3 = 2.93

$$PI_M = \frac{2.85 + 3.16 + 2.93}{3} = \frac{8.94}{3} = 2.98$$

3. Computation of standard deviation (s) for prevalence index (PI):

$$s = \sqrt{\frac{(PI_1 - PI_M)^2 + (PI_2 - PI_M)^2 + (PI_3 - PI_M)^2}{N - 1}}$$

For example:

Transect	PI_i	PI_M	$(PI_i - PI_M)$	$(PI_i - PI_M)^2$
1	2.85	2.98	−0.13	0.0169
2	3.16	2.98	0.18	0.0324
3	2.93	2.98	−0.05	0.0025
				0.0518

$$s = \sqrt{\frac{0.0518}{3-1}} = \sqrt{\frac{0.0518}{2}} = \sqrt{0.0259} = 0.161$$

4. Computation of standard error ($\bar{s}x$) of the prevalence index:

$$\bar{s}x = \frac{s}{\sqrt{N}} = \frac{0.161}{\sqrt{3}} = \frac{0.161}{1.73} = 0.093$$

Since 0.093 does not exceed 0.20, no additional transects are needed.

5. Record mean prevalence index value.

$$PI_M = 2.98$$

Since 2.98 is less than 3.0, the area has hydrophytic vegetation. If the wetland hydrology criterion is met, then the area is a wetland.

www.ingramcontent.com/pod-product-compliance
Lightning Source LLC
Chambersburg PA
CBHW080257290526
45790CB00005B/1846